The Future of the Republican Party

ALSO BY ROBERT J. DONOVAN

The Assassins   1955

Eisenhower: The Inside Story   1956

My First Fifty Years in Politics,
as Told to Robert J. Donovan
(autobiography of Joseph W. Martin, Jr.)   1960

PT 109: John F. Kennedy in World War II   1961

The
Future of the
Republican
Party

by Robert J. Donovan

AN NAL-WORLD BOOK
Published by The New American Library

First Printing
Library of Congress Catalog Card No.: 64–66377
Published by The New American Library of World Literature, Inc.
501 Madison Avenue, New York, New York 10022
Published simultaneously in Canada by
General Publishing Company, Ltd.
Printed in the United States of America

To my sister, Katherine

Foreword

THE NOMINATION of Senator Barry Goldwater for President last July was an event that was bound to have a wide effect on the character and destiny of the Republican party. It reversed the liberal trend of Republican Presidential nominations that had prevailed for a quarter of a century. It set the Republican party, at least temporarily, on a new course. It opened the floodgates of factionalism. Finally, as soon became apparent, it put the party once more on the road to defeat, which meant that after election day the Republicans would have to fight the battle of San Francisco over again in a long, tortured struggle to find the soul of the party and to redefine its purposes.

Since all these circumstances were quite evident soon after the San Francisco convention, it struck me that this was a uniquely good opportunity to take a fresh look at the Republican party. It was the right moment to pore over its history, to take a critical look at its campaign in 1964, and with the help of the best minds I could find, to try to glimpse what might lie ahead.

Accordingly, on an assignment from the Los Angeles *Times* I spent nearly three months traveling about the country talking to politicians and scholars alike. I interviewed former Republican national chairmen, incumbent state chairmen and national committeemen, local campaign officials, and officeholders high and low. In hopes of getting a broader perspective I spent almost as much time around the

American-history and political-science departments of colleges and universities as I did around political headquarters. To get a firsthand look at the campaign I traveled briefly with Senator Goldwater and President Johnson.

I have drawn extensively on the historical works of Samuel Eliot Morison and Henry Steele Commager, George H. Mayer, the late V. O. Key, Jr., Malcolm C. Moos, Arthur Schlesinger, Jr., Alexander Heard, James MacGregor Burns, Clinton Rossiter, Donald S. Strong, and others and also on a variety of studies and papers, including Thomas E. Dewey's lectures at the Woodrow Wilson School of Public and International Affairs of Princeton University in 1950.

The nature of this book is reportorial. It grew out of a series of post-election articles in the Los Angeles *Times*. It is the product of an independent inquiry into the best opinion I could find on the present plight and future course of the Republican party.

Robert J. Donovan

Washington, D. C.
December, 1964

The Future of the Republican Party

1

THE Republican party has gone through a shattering time, but it is not shattered.

The devastating defeat of Barry Goldwater at the hands of the voters in all sections of the country but the Deep South has damaged, weakened, and tarnished the party. For years to come, as a result, the two-party system will be crippled, but it will not disappear. Though a savage fight for control of the party already has begun, the Republican party will survive. For at this stage of American history the two major parties are practically indestructible.

"Each one," as Professor Clinton Rossiter of Cornell wrote in *Parties and Politics in America*, "is a citadel that can withstand the impact of even the most disastrous national landslide and thus provide elements of obstinacy and stability in the two-party system."

The two-party system not only will survive but also will probably survive without any drastic national realignment between the two existing parties. The history of the Republican party suggests that its rightful role is that of the party of enlightened conservatism. The lesson of the 1964 election, written bold in the returns, is that it cannot successfully play this role, much less play it in the White House, until it casts off the extreme-right-wing conservatism of Senator Goldwater and his faction.

The Republican party, taken at its best, has a great history. It forced the slavery issue. It saved the Union. It is the party of the Emancipation Proclamation and the Thirteenth Amendment, freeing the slaves. It is the party that brought the United States, in the decades after the Civil War, to a position of preeminence among the industrial powers of the world. Under Republican administrations the West was opened, the transcontinental railroads were built, the Panama Canal was dug, the Homestead and the Sherman anti-trust acts were passed, the atoms-for-peace program was born, and programs for urban renewal and interstate highways were brought to fruition.

Taken at its best, it is a party that has harbored men of high stature: Abraham Lincoln, Theodore Roosevelt, Charles Evans Hughes, Henry L. Stimson, Elihu Root, the elder La Follette, the Tafts, and George Norris, to mention only some of those who have passed into history.

Traditions coming down from these men and these events have bequeathed durability to the Republican party. The very designation "Republican party," like "Democratic party," denotes an enduring entity. Each is a symbol, a fixture with a lasting meaning. The Republican emblem is of enduring value in elections. That is why politicians like New York's Governor Nelson A. Rockefeller and Pennsylvania's Governor William W. Scranton felt it necessary technically to endorse Goldwater, even though they deeply disapproved of his policies. They wanted to keep their credentials as Republicans in order in case they should seek to run again.

Two parties constitute a natural mechanism for providing alternatives. It is a mechanism rooted deep in the American past, and no third party has ever prevailed against it for long. If not the intent, at least the effect of the American constitutional system has been to foster the existence of two major parties in a way that would have been impossible under, for example, a system of proportional representation. The political scientist C. A. Berdahl summed the matter up well when he wrote, "The two-party system is so much a

2

part of our governmental and political structure that it need not be argued, not explained, nor even understood; it is like the Constitution and the Monroe Doctrine, something we accept as a matter of course."

Republicans who wonder in the wake of the Goldwater debacle whether their party may now be going the way of the Whigs may remember with some consolation that for a century this has been an oft-asked question after election day. After Alfred E. Smith lost to Herbert Hoover in 1928, Silas Bent, a former publicity director of the Democratic National Committee, wrote a gloomy article for *Scribner's* called "Will the Democrats Follow the Whigs?" And the Whigs were much on the Republican mind after Alfred M. Landon's defeat by Franklin D. Roosevelt in 1936.

Bad as the Goldwater defeat was, it was not, at least on a numerical basis, as sweeping as the 1936 landslide. Out of the wreckage of Landon's hopes the Republican party salvaged only eight votes out of five hundred and thirty-one in the electoral college, eight governors in the forty-eight states, seventeen seats out of ninety-six in the Senate, and eighty-nine seats out of four hundred and thirty-five in the House of Representatives. People asked if the party was dead. Yet the party not only lived, but soon made a remarkable resurgence. In the congressional elections of 1938 the Republicans picked up six seats in the Senate and seventy-one in the House. Roosevelt was thrown on the defensive, so much so that he might not have been elected to a third term in 1940 if war had not broken out in Europe. But even with this psychological advantage to the Democrats, Wendell L. Willkie received 22,304,755 votes.

Roughly 22,000,000 votes were cast for Thomas E. Dewey in each of his losing campaigns, 1944 and 1948. The total vote for Dwight D. Eisenhower reached 33,936,252 in 1952 and 35,585,316 in 1956. In defeat Richard M. Nixon received 34,108,546 in 1960. And for all his drawbacks, Senator Goldwater got more than 26,000,000 votes.

These various votes mentioned above were not, except in Eisenhower's case, enough to provide a Republican victory. But they provided a vast source of political capital for the Republican party on which it has been able to keep venturing forth in quest of victory.

Throughout the last decade the Republicans have polled a large vote in the congressional elections even though they did not succeed in winning control of Congress. In these elections their percentage of the popular vote was 47 in 1954, 48.7 in 1956, 43.4 in 1958, 44.8 in 1960, and 47.2 in 1962.

Even while losing the Presidency and control of the House and Senate in 1964, the Republicans managed to elect seven senators, giving them a total of thirty-two members of the Senate. They elected one hundred and forty representatives and eight governors. Altogether there are now seventeen Republican governors, including governors of such important states as New York, Ohio, Michigan, Pennsylvania, Oregon, Oklahoma, and Kansas.

In addition to these Republican officeholders at the top, the party has councilmen, selectmen, county clerks, assemblymen, state senators, and thousands of lesser officials throughout the country.

Millions of Republicans work for the party's candidates and contribute money to its campaigns. Loyalties, in the Republican as well as the Democratic party, are remarkably persistent. "Attachments to partisan labels," as the distinguished political scientist V. O. Key, Jr., noted, "live long beyond the events that gave them birth." Normally the Republican party enjoys the support of a majority of American newspaper owners and publishers. It is usually the party of the most powerful business and financial interests in the country. Although it is not the party of intellectuals its ranks include a large number of educated men and women.

These are all elements of strength that only a major party can possess. Although the Republican party is now in an atrocious state, still it has sinews built by a long history, great names, a large and educated following, numerous officeholders in most parts of the country, bountiful sources of wealth, editorial support, and an enduring emblem.

It is true that the party was abnormally weakened in 1964 by the defection of millions of Republicans to the Democratic ticket. But this is not necessarily or even probably a permanent loss. Periodic defection is a common occurrence in American politics. Eisenhower was swept into office on a wave that included so many Democratic votes that it first appeared that a major political shift might be in the making, restoring the Republican party to its former status as majority party. At the close of the Eisenhower administration the Democrats were returned to power in 1960, however close the popular vote, by an electoral vote of three hundred and three to two hundred and nineteen.

Victory by a landslide is no guarantee of success four years later. Grover Cleveland's triumph in 1892, for example, was thought to be decisive, a forerunner of prolonged Democratic rule. Yet in 1896 William McKinley put the Republicans back in the White House, where they were to remain for twenty-eight of the next thirty-six years. Hoover's resounding defeat of Smith in 1928 was followed by Roosevelt's resounding defeat of Hoover in 1932. The truest saying in politics, as valid now as ever, is that four years is a long time.

If ever there was an election in recent years in which a true political realignment might have been expected, it was the election of 1964 because of the nomination of a candidate at the extreme-right end of the spectrum. After he was nominated, however, Senator Goldwater made certain significant gestures to the liberal Republican viewpoint that tended to keep the party together. At the Republican conference in Hershey, Pennsylvania, in August, 1964, he disavowed extremism, declared his support of the United Nations, and promised that if elected he would not appoint the Secretaries of State and of Defense without consulting Eisenhower and Nixon. And with regard to domestic policy he promised in the formal opening of his campaign in Prescott, Arizona, to "honor the commitments the government has made to all areas of the economy. We must," he said, "proceed with care in our task of cutting the government down to size."

Throughout the campaign he kept emphasizing that he would not sell the Tennessee Valley Authority, abolish Social Security, or scrap farm price-supports. True, his previous and seemingly contradictory statements on these matters had already done him irreparable harm. The point is, however, that by and large the drift of his campaign was away from extreme positions that could have forced such a cataclysmic Republican split as would have threatened some major realignment.

Within limits, of course, a constant process of realignment goes on between the parties; the process was probably more diffuse in 1964 than in other years. Doubtless there will be changes ensuing from the Johnson-Goldwater election that will be felt for a long time.

It is possible, for example, that the extreme-right wing may split away from the Republican party and form a third party, as the Gold Democrats did in 1896 and the Dixiecrats did in 1948 when they bolted the Democratic National Convention in Philadelphia. Governor George C. Wallace of Alabama would dearly love to lead such a party. It is possible that, having voted for Goldwater in 1964, the Dixiecrat states of 1948 might now organize as the Republican Dixiecrats. After all, their 1948 Presidential nominee, Senator Strom Thurmond of South Carolina, turned Republican in time to help Goldwater carry that state in 1964. Surely he would be ready and willing to lead the Republican Dixiecrats.

Regardless of the extraordinary character of the 1964 election, nothing that has happened indicates a major, nationwide realignment, such as the long-dreamed-of shift bringing all liberals into the Democratic party and all conservatives into the Republican party. There was the single notable example of Thurmond's switch from the Democratic to the Republican party, but this was a petty, sectional matter. No broad movements developed that carried Senators Clifford Case, Thomas H. Kuchel, and Jacob K. Javits, for example, into the Democratic party, or Senators Spessard L. Holland, James O. Eastland, and Harry F. Byrd into the Republican party. Even those who, like Senator Richard B. Russell of Georgia, favor such a realignment and consider it inevitable do not know how it can be achieved.

"Both parties have a big left wing and a big right wing," Russell has said, "and both of them are oil and water."

It will be fortunate for the Republican party if no such realignment occurs. As Thomas E. Dewey said in his lectures at Princeton in 1950: "These impractical theorists . . . want to drive all the moderates and liberals out of the Republican party and have the remainder join forces with the conservative groups of the South. Then they would have everything neatly arranged indeed. The Democratic party would be the liberal-to-radical party. The Republican party would be the conservative-to-reactionary party. The results would be neatly arranged too. The Republicans would lose every election, and the Democrats would win every election. It may be a perfect theory but it would result in a one-party system. . . ."

"The unwritten laws of American politics," says Clinton Rossiter, "demand that the parties overlap substantially in principle, policy, character, appeal, and purpose—or cease to be parties with any hope of winning a national election."

The recent election is a fine case in point.

The Republican party will survive the Goldwater crash. In all likelihood it will survive in familiar form without any radical realignment. When its many elements of strength in the communities, the states, and the country at large are

7

taken into account, it remains a vast organization and a vital force in the United States.

"Americans have always been tenacious in their party allegiance," George H. Mayer wrote in *The Republican Party 1854–1964.* "Long periods of one-party supremacy have been the rule rather than the exception."

Because the Democrats made pronounced gains in the 1964 congressional elections, the Republicans probably will begin making a comeback of sorts in the congressional elections of 1966. Historically the party out of power gains in off-year elections. Barring the most unusual circumstances, it is unlikely that the Democrats will increase their majorities in Congress in 1966.

Nevertheless, when all this has been granted, the fact remains that the Republican party suffered a devastating blow in 1964 and now faces one of the worst crises in its entire history.

Except for the eight years of the Eisenhower administration, which was less than a true test of party strength because of the unique esteem in which the general was held then, the Republicans have been out of the White House since 1932. Their standing in Congress has been even sorrier. Only one Republican Speaker of the House has been elected since Nicholas Longworth, who died during the Hoover administration. His solitary successor was Representative Joseph W. Martin, Jr., of Massachusetts, who presided over the only two sessions in which the Republicans have controlled Congress since 1930. These were the celebrated Eightieth Congress, in 1947–48, during the Truman administration; and the Eighty-third Congress, in 1953–54, during the Eisenhower administration.

On election day, 1964, the Republicans again failed to regain control, so they will be out of power in the House for at least another two years. And while they may pick up some seats in 1966, there are no circumstances apparent today that suggest they can recapture control of Congress then.

The election of 1968 is too far in the distance to make any forecasts about the makeup of the House. But regardless of what happens in the House, it is not likely that the Republicans can regain control of the Senate even in 1968, because of the present numerical superiority of Democratic senators and because of the large number of ordinarily safe Southern Democratic seats that will be at stake in 1966 and 1968.

Thus, as in all but four of the last thirty-four years, the Democrats will continue to control congressional committees that pass upon federal appropriations; federal taxes; federal appointments, including judgeships; foreign policy; military policy; farm policy; nuclear policy; space policy; trade policy; and civil-rights and immigration legislation. Almost as important from the political point of view perhaps is the fact that the Democrats will continue to control committees that conduct investigations, therefore having the principal say as to who and what shall be investigated by Congress and how far such investigations shall probe.

With each year that passes fewer Republicans remain who have had important experience in handling the affairs of the United States government at home and abroad. Already the Republicans have been in the opposition so long that many of them have forgotten the great traditions of the party, as the San Francisco convention so garishly demonstrated.

Herbert Hoover is dead, and by 1968 millions of voters will not be able to remember firsthand any Republican President other than General Eisenhower. Young voters who will be going to the polls for the first time will remember John F. Kennedy much more vividly.

One by one, with each Presidential term that the Democrats have won in this generation, the great interests of the country—business, labor, finance, agriculture, science, and so on—have become progressively more accustomed to dealing with a Democratic administration. How far the mutual adjustment and accommodation have gone has been strikingly clear in the very first year of President Lyndon B. Johnson's tenure. If the trend of the last thirty years continues, the Democratic party will be regarded as the party of government, to its own detriment in many ways, but also at great danger to the vigor and influence of the Republican party.

In the wake of the latest Republican defeat, in which Goldwater carried only six small states, a plausible projection could be made showing the Democrats retaining control of the White House at least until 1988, thus approaching the fifty-six years of Republican supremacy in the seventy-two-year period beginning with Lincoln and ending with Hoover. Roughly this projection presumes President Johnson's winning a second full term in 1968, after which would come the election and reelection of Hubert H. Humphrey in 1972 and 1976, followed perhaps by Robert or Edward Kennedy in 1980 and 1984.

Though the likelihood of it is questionable because of fate, the suddenness of change, and the pendulum swings of American public opinion, the idea is not preposterous, particularly if the Republican party remains hopelessly divided for many years between the left and right wings, as may be the case. The fact that even the possibility of such a long reign by the Democrats is seriously discussed by able political scientists and astute politicians demonstrates what a sad condition the Republican party is thought to be in.

The persistent Democratic victories, especially the surprising election of Harry S Truman in 1948 and the hairbreadth triumph of Kennedy in 1960, clearly suggest that it will take a political upheaval or the appearance of an unusual candidate like Eisenhower to oust the Democrats. Republicans will be on the safe side in assuming that President Johnson will use his new victory shrewdly. On the one hand he will interpret it as a mandate to go forward in the fields of civil-rights enforcement, medical care for the elderly, federal assistance to education, and the reduction of poverty. On the other hand he will mix in an assortment of conservative measures to appeal to the Republicans who supported him. On top of all he will set out to become a great figure on the international stage. There is good reason to believe that Johnson will be an effective President and one who will devote incredible energy to the strengthening of the Democratic party.

The 1964 election was evidence enough of the power the Republicans are up against, in part because of their split over Goldwater. Behind the President was not only the old winning F.D.R. coalition of racial, ethnic, and religious minorities; labor, white-collar workers, and intellectuals; and (though to a much smaller extent) the South, but an entirely new element as well. This is the important section of the business and financial community that supported the Democratic nominee.

Coalitions, especially large ones of this kind with many conflicting interests, are hard to hold together. Nothing is surer, however, than that Johnson will cater to business and will employ all his skills and go to great lengths to keep his new allies under the tent. The Republicans will be in deep trouble if they have to contend with a Democratic administration based on the broad masses of voters and the support of both business and labor and the blessings of the intellectuals.

The election accentuated Democratic strengths and Republican weaknesses. Already the majority party by a great length, the Democrats picked up a much larger percentage of newly registered voters than the Republicans. When a person registers in a party, he does not thereby make a commitment to vote for its candidates. Registrations do, however, indicate a voting trend. Thus the new voters who registered Democratic in 1964 may be a reservoir of potential new strength in future elections.

The Democrats increased their hold on allies among the racial, ethnic, and religious groups. More Negroes voted for

Johnson than for Kennedy. More Jews voted for Johnson than for Kennedy. Even more Catholics voted for Johnson than for Kennedy.

Though it lost Alabama, Mississippi, Louisiana, South Carolina, and Georgia in 1964, the Democratic party ran stronger in Texas than in 1960, and, besides winning North Carolina and Arkansas, recaptured Virginia, Florida, and Tennessee, which Nixon had carried in 1960. Johnson was the first Democratic Presidential nominee to carry California since 1948.

The Democrats won the greatest majority in the House of Representatives since the New Deal heyday of 1936. In New York State, once a mighty Democratic bastion, they recaptured control of the state legislature for the first time in more than a quarter of a century. With Robert F. Kennedy as the new United States senator from New York, there is a good prospect that the sorry mess in which the Democratic organization has wallowed in New York for years will be rectified in time to make it difficult for Rockefeller or any other Republican to win the governorship in 1966.

The Republicans were grievously weakened. Their historic influence in New England and the Midwest continued to wane. Vermont, which had withstood even the Roosevelt landslide of 1936, went Democratic for the first time in history. Maine voted for a Democratic President for the first time since Woodrow Wilson carried it in the Bull Moose split of 1912. Connecticut finally became more Democratic than the Georgia of a decade ago. Half the Republicans in New England bolted the party in 1964, and for the first time all the New England states landed in the Democratic column.

In the Midwest the Republicans lost Kansas and Indiana for the first time since 1936. Two upcoming young Republicans who might have been important rallying points in the rebuilding of the party—Representative Robert A. Taft, Jr., of Ohio, who was defeated in his race for the U.S. Senate, and Charles H. Percy, chairman and chief executive officer of the Bell & Howell Company, who lost out in his bid for the governorship of Illinois—were lost in the Democratic tidal wave that swept over the entire Midwest.

The rejection of Goldwater by millions of Republican voters in the suburbs undercut the party in the one area of American life that had seemed to hold the most promise for it. It was even deserted by the farmers of the Great Plains, once a sturdy bulwark of support.

Town and country, city and suburb, black and white, rich and poor, Catholic, Protestant, and Jew voted for President Johnson on November 3, 1964.

The nomination of Senator Goldwater made it as certain as anything in politics can be that the Republicans would take a dreadful licking. Probably they would have lost no matter whom they ran, but the nomination of a right-wing conservative at this moment in history all but guaranteed disaster. Another candidate might have lost without leaving the Republican party in the shambles it is today.

The Goldwater nomination was the culmination of a long string of errors, miscalculation, folly, bad luck, and missed opportunities that have plagued the Republican party for the last half century. "From time to time in our history," Tom Dewey once remarked in the rueful aftermath of his own misfortune, "one party or the other has enjoyed a long period of ascendancy because it has grasped an opportunity or because the other has miscalculated."

For more than a generation now that party of ascendancy has been the Democratic party, and it has been so for both of the reasons mentioned by Dewey, namely, alertness to its own opportunities and miscalculation by the opposition.

In 1964, as has been the case in most of the campaigns since 1932, the Republicans were simply unable to find a winning issue. On top of that, Senator Goldwater ran a campaign that was so bad that it was difficult to regard him as a serious candidate for President of the United States.

The Republicans chased after a will-o'-the-wisp of conservative votes that were waiting for a genuine conservative in a never-never land first suspected by the late Senator Robert A. Taft but never yet discovered. As had been true throughout the history of this century, the Republicans once more failed to identify themselves with the interests of the masses of people. And as has been just as true, the Republicans could not make up their mind what, as a party, they really stood for.

2

THE HEAVY DEFEAT suffered in 1964 by the Republicans, already four years out of power, was due in no small measure to the split personality that has afflicted the party for many years.

The schizophrenia at San Francisco was only the nastiest chapter in the long story of an ideological division that has persistently shaken the Republican party to its foundations. It is one of the basic causes of the adversity and failure the Republicans have experienced in the twentieth century in contrast to their prosperity in the nineteenth.

From the Bull Moose to Barry Goldwater the party has at critical moments tended to pull in opposite directions. The Republican liberals and the Republican conservatives hate each other more than they hate Democrats.

The conservatives could not stomach Willkie or Dewey or Rockefeller. The liberals, or "moderates," abhorred Goldwater. Their rejection of his philosophy left its mark on the outcome of the 1964 election, as millions of Republicans stayed home and other millions voted for President Johnson.

In one state after another—in New York, in New Jersey, in Michigan, in all the New England states—Republicans generally refused to bestir themselves to help Goldwater against Johnson; in many other states they did only what was needed to meet the minimum requirements of party loyalty. The Republican who won the largest victory on election day, Governor George Romney of Michigan, had refused even to endorse Goldwater, as had other prominent moderates like Senator Kenneth B. Keating and Representative John V. Lindsay of New York.

This split is a disease of the Republican mind that nothing seems able to purge, neither a victory like Eisenhower's in 1952 nor a defeat like Goldwater's in 1964. After Eisenhower had defeated the conservatives at the Republican National Convention in Chicago in 1952, the conservatives in their positions of power in Congress proceeded to thwart him when he entered the White House. After the defeat of Goldwater on November 3, 1964, the battle of San Francisco began breaking out again.

The returns were barely in before Goldwater's campaign manager, Denison Kitchel, said, "We may have to wait for four years, but we're going to get this government back to where it belongs." The morning after his defeat Goldwater said, "This effort we engaged in . . . turns out to be a much longer effort than we thought. It's not an effort that we can drop now, nor do we have any intentions of dropping it now." A day later Governor Nelson A. Rockefeller said, "It is time for the Republican party to return to the principles upon which it was founded and upon which the Republican party and America achieved greatness." Governor William W. Scranton said that the time had come for the party to "return to its heritage." Senator Jacob K. Javits of New York said that the "radical views" of Goldwater were responsible for the Johnson landslide and urged that Goldwater step aside as titular leader. Obviously the Republican party is again floundering in the confusion of aims that has been its hallmark in this century.

What *does* the Republican party stand for? Does it stand for internationalism or nationalism? Does it stand for the use of federal power to serve humane ends or does it stand for reliance primarily on the states and private institutions to take care of human needs? Is it for or against the TVA, foreign aid, the nuclear-test-ban treaty, the civil-rights act of 1964, and medical care for the elderly? Does it look forward or does it look backward?

Is it the party of Theodore Roosevelt or William Howard Taft? The party of Willkie, Dewey, and Eisenhower or the party of the late Robert A. Taft? The party of Rockefeller, Scranton, Javits, and Henry Cabot Lodge, Jr., or the party of Senator Goldwater? The party of old-line congressional leaders, past and present, like Styles Bridges, Owen Brewster, Hamilton Fish, Kenneth Wherry, Charles A. Halleck, Joseph W. Martin, Jr., John Taber, Dan Reed, and John W. Bricker or the party of Earl Warren, Thomas H. Kuchel, John Sherman Cooper, and Leverett M. Saltonstall?

The fratricide at San Francisco last July, which contributed so greatly to the ruins now spread about, differed only in degree from the way Republicans had been treating one another for a long time. The booing of Rockefeller and Javits in the Cow Palace would not have seemed out of place at the Chicago convention of 1912, where William Howard Taft's followers distributed handbills announcing that the former President of the United States, Colonel Roosevelt, would walk upon the waters of Lake Michigan at seven-thirty o'clock the next evening.

When the Republicans met in Chicago in 1912 they had, barring Grover Cleveland's two terms, been in residence in the White House since 1860. After the split in Chicago the party was never the same. In the fifty-two years that have followed, Republicans have occupied the White House for only twenty years. The results of the 1964 election make it difficult to say when they might be expected to return.

Historically the Democratic party too has been divided on the civil-rights issue. Every four years, however, the Democrats have had the genius to mitigate their differences sufficiently to get through the convention and the campaign with unity enough to make them formidable on election day. Their division is sectional, horizontal.

The fierce and costly conflict between Republican con-

17

servatives and liberals is a vertical slash through the party in practically all sections. It cuts like a canyon through the map of Republican history of the last half century. Its jagged course points the way to where the party stands today. The clash of the Goldwater movement and the liberals in 1964 was like a distant echo of the Bull Moose split.

Then as now the conservatives talked a different language from the liberals, or as they called themselves at that time, the Progressives. Taft praised the restrictive Payne-Aldrich tariff act. Ignoring the Progressives, he moved over to the side of the Old Guard in Congress. A quarrel within the administration led him to dismiss Gifford Pinchot, the conservationist, a hero in the eyes of many liberals to this day. Refusing to read newspapers that criticized him, Taft snapped, "I don't care what the other side is doing."

The Progressives of 1912 sounded like New Dealers a generation ahead of their time, which is to say they sounded the way the liberal Republicans of today sound to the conservative Republicans. The Progressives clamored for modern methods of dealing with the industrial revolution. They went far beyond the conservatives in advocating federal intervention for this purpose. They favored wider executive power to promote the general welfare. They wanted broader definition of the rights of labor. They insisted that the government exercise more regulation of big business and big finance. They called for preservation of national resources and imposition of the graduated income tax and the inheritance tax.

How can one catch the quintessence of the conflicting philosophies within the Republican party as they have come down through the decades? The best example that comes to mind is the contrast between Goldwater's attacks on the breadth of Supreme Court decisions in the field of human rights and Theodore Roosevelt's famous speech at Osawatomie, Kansas, demanding of the judiciary "that it shall be

18

interested primarily in human welfare rather than in property."

When Roosevelt bolted the party at Chicago, he took its best brains with him. The defection of the Progressives ended all chance of liberalizing the Republican party in that generation. The Republican split elected Woodrow Wilson in 1912. By the end of his administration Wilson had attracted to the Democratic party a long line of idealists, intellectuals, and liberals from whose influence and that of their successors it benefits to this day.

In the decade of the 1920's the division in the party was papered over by the profits of Wall Street and the bonanza of real estate. Still, the legacy of the Harding, Coolidge, and Hoover administrations was politically damaging to the Republican party. The Harding administration scandals left a deep stain. Furthermore, Harding and Coolidge in particular lost touch with realities at home and abroad, and Hoover was overwhelmed by the Great Depression.

Even when Hoover had won in 1928, eclipsing Alfred E. Smith by four hundred and forty-four electoral votes to eighty-seven, trouble was descending on the Republicans that few perceived at the time. In 1924 the Republicans had carried the dozen largest cities by 1,300,000 votes. In 1928, despite their poor showing in the electoral college, the Democrats carried these same cities by small margins. The Democratic inroads into the Republican North had begun. The trend was brought to fruition in Roosevelt's victory over Hoover in 1932, transforming the Democratic party at last into the majority party.

It was then, when the Democrats came back into power and under Roosevelt put through the huge New Deal programs, that the old split reappeared in the Republican party. It deepened as the issue of isolationism gripped the country with the approach of World War II.

"The inauguration of Roosevelt on March 4, 1933," says George H. Mayer, "marked the beginning of an era which

19

was to prove as disheartening for the Republican party as the post-Civil War decades had been for the Democrats. The unfamiliar frustrations of minority status embittered GOP leaders, clouded their judgment, and goaded them into political errors. Each blunder led to mutual recriminations and the deterioration of morale, which in turn provoked fresh disaster at the polls. Like a groggy, bewildered football team, the Republicans never escaped from the shadows of their own goal post. In their hour of adversity all their sins of omission in the 1920's were there to plague them.

"Having limited the party to the role of custodian of prosperity, the Republicans lacked principles which could be employed to slow down defections during the Depression. No pressure group but big business remained loyal, and its continued support became a liability when congressional investigations uncovered a multitude of dishonest financial transactions dating back to the hectic days before the stock market crash."

By the time of the 1934 congressional elections the Republicans were hard at it again, this time squabbling among themselves over the line of attack on the New Deal.

Hoover, hoping to be renominated in 1936, favored an across-the-board indictment of Roosevelt and his program. He wrote a book proclaiming the New Deal to be a dictatorship and went about the country calling on the people to save the Constitution by voting for the Republicans. The Republican congressional leaders, whose mail kept them keenly aware of the popularity of the New Deal, were afraid that Hoover's strategy would boomerang. The predecessors of today's Republican moderates began to see a place for New Deal reforms in the world of the mid-twentieth century. They perceived that the party might safely oppose the means but not the ends of many of Roosevelt's policies.

A number of Republicans who were up for reelection in 1934 therefore split with Hoover. They frankly told their constituents they were sympathetic to the aims of the New

Deal. Some of them, like Senator Hiram Johnson of California and Senator Robert M. La Follette, Jr., of Wisconsin, actually sought and received Roosevelt's endorsement. On election day the Democrats won by a bigger landslide than in 1932 and became the first party in power since 1866 to increase its margins in both houses in an off-year election.

At the 1936 convention in Cleveland the Republicans shouted themselves hoarse over Hoover's uncompromising attack on the New Deal, but they nominated Alfred M. Landon, the son of a Bull Mooser, and adopted a platform whose underlying theme was, in Mayer's words, "one of capitulation to a new order."

After Landon's crushing defeat the Republicans once more fell to feuding among themselves. Landon and Hoover disagreed bitterly over the course the party should follow. The former President regarded the 1936 returns as a personal vindication and maneuvered to seize control of the party from those liberals around Landon who had dabbled in New Deal philosophies. Hoover got the idea of calling a midterm Republican convention, a proposal that has been revived here and there since the Goldwater debacle, but Landon, sensing that it would be a vehicle for an attempted Hoover comeback, thwarted it. The only thing all Republicans could agree upon, it seems, was opposing Roosevelt's court-packing bill. Even this was not enough to hold them together, particularly after such events as the march of Hitler's troops abroad and the rise of Wendell Willkie at home. By the time the Republican National Convention opened in Philadelphia in 1940 the party was sundered by the deepest split since 1912.

"The Republican party," wrote Walter Lippmann at the time of the convention, "is at present too much divided and confused to take a clear position on any great question."

Philadelphia was to be the first of three historic conventions—those of 1940, 1948, and 1952—in which the party was shaken to its roots by the futile struggle of angry conservatives to wrench the nomination away from candidates backed by Eastern interests.

A four-cornered contest at first, the 1940 convention narrowed to a showdown between Willkie and Senator Robert A. Taft. Willkie had swept into Philadelphia with powerful connections among the financial and business interests of the East and the fervid support of publishers like Henry R. Luce, the Cowles brothers, Roy Howard, and the Reids of the New York *Herald Tribune*. Taft was the favorite of Hoover's conservative followers and of a great many Republicans in Congress. Forty of the latter issued a manifesto appealing to the convention not to nominate Willkie, who had previously been a registered Democrat. In spite of the frantic efforts of the conservatives, Willkie, the "outsider" supported by the East, was nominated on the sixth ballot. The schism within the party was embittered by the news that Roosevelt, in a masterpiece of timing, had appointed to his Cabinet two eminent Republicans—Henry L. Stimson, who earlier had served in the Cabinets of two Republican Presidents, and Frank Knox, the Chicago publisher who had been Landon's running mate in 1936. As if the party were not divided enough, an effort was made to put through the convention a resolution reading Stimson and Knox out of the party. Cooler heads finally prevented it.

Nevertheless, after losing the nomination, Taft returned to Washington and staged a hostile interrogation of Stimson when his appointment as Secretary of War came up for confirmation before the Senate Committee on Military Affairs, of which Taft was not even a member. Stimson, who had once been Secretary of War in the Cabinet of the senator's father, thoroughly resented the unfriendly questioning.

By then the issue of isolation was dividing Republicans even more deeply than had the old issues of economic liberalism and conservatism, though the contending factions were roughly the same as they had been in the past and were to continue to be down to the present time.

Following his nomination, Willkie had great difficulty choosing a new Republican national chairman who would be acceptable to both wings—roughly, the wing backed by the interventionist *Herald Tribune* and the wing backed by the isolationist Chicago *Tribune*. As a compromise he eventually picked Joseph Martin, then the Republican leader of the House, whose votes placed him among the isolationists, though personally he was a rather mild one.

In short order, however, Willkie found himself going one way and the Republicans in Congress going another on vital issues like selective service and the lease of destroyers to Great Britain in return for bases. The Eastern press and Eastern business leaders generally supported Willkie in his endorsement of Roosevelt's proposals for aiding the Allies, short of war. Midwestern Republicans, who were powerful in Congress, clamorously opposed him.

"If I had been Demosthenes," Martin said in his memoirs, "I could not have reversed this powerful Republican sentiment in the House. There was no possible way of holding the Republican forces together except by accommodating it. To have tried to align the body of Republican Representatives behind Roosevelt's foreign policies, even if I had been of a mind to do so, would have torn the Republican organization in the House to tatters."

Hoover, Landon, and Taft all opposed lend-lease. When Willkie testified in favor of it, he incurred a tirade from members of his own party in Congress. Within a year of Willkie's nomination the second-ranking Republican on the House Military Affairs Committee, Representative Dewey Short of Missouri, rose in the House and characterized him as "Wee Windy War Willkie—a Bellowing, Blatant, Bellicose, Belligerent, Bombastic Blowhard." Willkie's own brand of liberalism was soon repudiated by his fellow Republicans in Congress. Senator Gerald P. Nye of North Dakota, a leading Republican isolationist, denounced him as a "betrayer" of the party. Only an appeal by Martin averted a resolution at the Des Moines meeting of the Young Republican National Federation in 1941 repudiating Willkie as a Republican voice on questions of foreign policy.

The fervor of the anti-Willkie isolationists cost the Republican party dearly, for after Pearl Harbor and the German declaration of war on the United States it was obvious that the course advocated by so many Republicans in Congress would have led to disaster.

"Not only did the bulk of Republicans vote indiscriminately against increased defense appropriations," says Mayer, "but they denied that America had any interests worth fighting for. In fact their mistrust of Roosevelt even drove some of them to speak well of America's potential enemies."

"At some point between 1932 and 1948," he added, "the Republicans might have won an election by capitalizing on the country's temporary weariness with familiar faces. Yet it is doubtful that they could have converted any great number of Democrats into Republicans on that basis. Their real opportunity during the New Deal era lay in the field of foreign policy, but they permitted the Democrats to make the most of isolationism while the issue was still popular, and then they clung to it with perverse stubbornness after it had ceased to have any real utility."

American entry into the war, and then, beginning soon after V-E Day, the sweeping Republican opposition to many of the policies of President Harry S Truman, quieted the intraparty quarrels until the 1948 convention in Philadelphia. The air of that convention was electric both with anger over the long tenure of the Democrats and with anticipation of a sweet Republican victory at last. "Let us waste no time measuring the unfortunate man in the White House against our specifications," Mrs. Clare Booth Luce told the delegates. "Mr. Truman's time is short; his situation is hopeless. Frankly, he is a gone goose." The nomination in that case was a one-way ticket to the White House, and the conservatives fought the liberals bitterly for it. Yet this time the conservatives fared even worse than in 1940. Dewey, the loser of the 1944 election, was nominated on the third ballot.

When Dewey went down to amazing defeat at the hands of the man from Independence, Missouri, the Republicans were thrown into a fit of frustration, which came to a head at the next convention, in 1952, in Chicago. By then a great many Republicans, especially Midwestern Republicans, were convinced beyond all persuasion that the successive defeats of Willkie in 1940 and Dewey in 1944 and 1948 practically proved that a liberal Republican was doomed to defeat. Forerunners of the Goldwater following of 1964, they believed passionately that the voters were waiting to swarm to the polls to elect an orthodox Republican who typified implacable opposition to the whole business of the New Deal and the Fair Deal. They could fairly smell victory for a conservative who would promise to cut taxes, reduce the burdens of Truman's costly containment policy in Korea and around the world, and weed out the Communists who were supposed to be infesting the government in Washington.

The man who fit this bill of particulars to perfection was, of course, "Mr. Republican," Senator Taft, by then a revered figure among the conservatives, who had gone to Chicago knowing it would be his last chance at the Presidential nomination. The challenge he faced was great, for the forces who had engineered the nomination of Willkie and Dewey had now produced Dwight D. Eisenhower, America's greatest war hero since Ulysses S. Grant.

The climactic scene at Chicago was the prelude to the drama in San Francisco in 1964. The orator was Everett McKinley Dirksen. The convention was on the verge of a test vote that would determine who would be nominated, Taft or Eisenhower.

"To my friends from New York," Dirksen intoned, "when

25

my friend Tom Dewey was the candidate in 1944 and 1948 (boos), I tried to be one of his best campaigners, and you ask him whether or not I didn't go into eighteen states one year and twenty-three states the next. Reexamine your hearts before you take this action. . . ."

He paused and slowly twirled his forefinger in the face of Dewey, the powerhouse of the Eisenhower forces, who was seated with the New York delegation. "We followed you before," Dirksen said, "and you took us down the path to defeat."

The conservative lament in a nutshell. It did not prevail at Chicago. The delegates wanted to give Taft the prize he had worked for so long, but a convention permeated with fear that Taft could not win nominated Eisenhower. But in their hearts the conservatives believed that Dirksen was right, and when the opportunity came twelve years later at San Francisco, they seized it.

If the twentieth century has been an unpropitious time for the Republicans, the middle years of it, beginning in 1948, have been the worst. For it was in this period that the party kicked away its greatest opportunities.

First Dewey lost the chance for the Republicans to move into the White House on January 20, 1949. Then when victory finally did come to the Republicans in 1952, President Eisenhower, with the considerable help of his associates in Congress, failed to build the party into the dominant party in the United States. Next Richard M. Nixon and the party in general failed to capitalize on the opportunity in 1960 to extend the Republican tenure in the White House. Finally, in 1964, the Republicans nominated Barry Goldwater, who had about as much chance of being elected President of the United States as would a splinter-party candidate, which in effect he was.

The 1948 defeat was a critical one. It led inexorably to new difficulties that undermined the party's strength for years. Ironically, the Republicans began laying the groundwork for this defeat in the course of winning, in the 1946 congressional elections, their greatest triumph up to that point since the election of Hoover. "Had enough?" they asked the voters in the fall of 1946. Fed up with war, government controls, and a meat shortage, the voters roared back, "Yes," and put the Republicans in control of both houses of the Eightieth Congress.

Rashly, the Republicans misread the returns to mean that the American people were ready to scrap most of the New Deal. Accordingly, the Eightieth Congress, for all its achievements, especially in the field of foreign policy, assumed under Taft's leadership an implacably anti-New Deal attitude. To the same jaded tune that had repelled voters in the thirties, it slashed appropriations for government services. It cut reclamation projects to ribbons. It turned a deaf ear to the appeals for help from Negroes who were migrating to the North. Perhaps worst of all, so far as Dewey's hopes went, it cut funds for the Commodity Credit Corporation, which meant that fewer cribs could be built for surplus-grain storage. In turn this forced farmers to sell at comparatively depressed prices, because with no place for storage they could not get government loans on their crops. Dewey refrained from defending the best of the record of the Eightieth Congress, and Truman saturated the country with denunciation of its failings. In winning the election Truman left the Republican party so demoralized that it fell back upon its worst elements. Having failed to dislodge the Democrats after twenty years, the Republicans fell prey to the kind of defeatism that is willing to try anything. The thing they finally seized upon in desperation was Senator Joseph McCarthy's brutality and character assassination. This grasp at any straw that would defeat and discredit Truman was accepted even by Senator Taft. At the height of McCarthy's assault upon the State Department in March, 1950, Taft was quoted by several reporters as having said that McCarthy should "keep talking and if one case doesn't work out he should proceed with another." If Dewey had won in 1948 this whole ugly era would have been averted because the Republicans would not have been frustrated. No one would have heard of McCarthy. Instead, the excesses of that period were to hound the party for years.

Eisenhower entered the White House in 1953 with personal power, glory, and claim upon the respect of the people unmatched since Roosevelt in his prime. What Roosevelt did for the Democratic party, however, Eisenhower did not even begin to do for the Republican party. He possessed neither the knowledge of how to do it nor the political thirst for doing it.

"Everything seems to have been patronage this morning," Eisenhower grumbled at the close of a cabinet meeting on October 9, 1953. Patronage was such a forbidding subject to the President that after the administration had been in office for some months Leonard W. Hall, the Republican national chairman, laconically reduced the staff of the patronage bureau at the National Committee headquarters to one or two persons. State and local Republican leaders were often outraged to learn from the newspapers about the appointment of Republicans in their respective areas to important jobs in the federal government.

This sort of thing was demoralizing to the Republican cadre, but it was insignificant compared with the unique opportunity Eisenhower passed up to bring Negroes back to the party. The year after he took office, the Supreme Court, under the leadership of Earl Warren, whom Eisenhower had appointed, held that racial segregation in the public schools was unconstitutional. This unloosed the historic tide that today has become a flood. Eisenhower might have lent his moral prestige to this decision and done much to see to it that, as the court prescribed, schools were integrated with all deliberate speed. Instead he and his Republican colleagues took a cold, if appropriate, legal view of

28

the whole matter. The President convinced many Negroes that he did not really care.

E. Frederick Morrow, a Negro who served on Eisenhower's staff, later wrote in his *Black Man in the White House* that Eisenhower's "lukewarm stand on civil rights made me heartsick. I could trust this man never to do anything that would jeopardize the civil rights and personal dignity of the American people, but it was obvious that he would never take any positive giant step to prove that he unequivocally stood for the right of every American to walk this land in dignity and peace. . . . His failure to clearly and forthrightly respond to the Negroes' plea for a strong position on civil rights was the greatest cross I had to bear in my years in Washington."

Eisenhower displayed no great interest in the gathering Negro revolution. In the Eisenhower years the Republican party truly might have become, as it was in Lincoln's time, the champion of Negro rights. It chose instead to let that role pass to John F. Kennedy and Lyndon B. Johnson, with results that the 1964 election have underscored dramatically.

The Republican history probably would have been different if Eisenhower had decided to limit his stay in the White House to one term and let Nixon run in 1956, before the Democrats had developed candidates like Kennedy, Johnson, and Humphrey. Nearly everything Eisenhower needed to do he did in his first term. He brought the Korean War to a close. He ended many of the divisions and hatreds that had seared the American people in the latter years of the Truman administration. If Eisenhower declined to take on McCarthy personally, at least he was the rock against which McCarthy was crushed. Eisenhower finally got the St. Lawrence Seaway bill through Congress and persuaded the Republicans to accept the domestic reforms of the Roosevelt-Truman era and to go along with the bipartisan foreign policy that had been in effect since the war. His second term was an anticlimax. Eisenhower's heart attack in

1955 gave him an acceptable reason for declining a second term. If Nixon had run against Adlai Stevenson in 1956 with Eisenhower's enthusiastic support, he might have won, whereupon he would have applied himself energetically to the building of the Republican party. It is quite probable in these several instances that the Democrats would not have been able to return to power in 1960.

Even in 1960 the momentum of the Eisenhower landslides might have carried Nixon into office if it had not been for costly mistakes. Nixon would not listen to good advice. He agreed to a series of televised debates with Kennedy, which resulted in giving the voters an entirely new and favorable impression of the young Democratic challenger. By making a fetish of campaigning in all fifty states, Nixon campaigned too little in states that were decisive. He failed, like so many other Republicans, to unite the conservatives and the liberals of the party. Then, in the end, his party somehow lacked the capacity to sustain the setbacks he had incurred.

Finally, a disappointing period in Republican history—a period of the lost opportunities of the Dewey campaign, the Eisenhower years in the White House and Nixon's near-miss—came to a climax in the nomination of Goldwater. The San Francisco convention simply pumped political adrenalin into tired Democratic veins. In truth, the Democrats had been running a little low on fresh issues. Even Herbert Hoover had at last ceased to be a scapegoat. The Democratic party was much in need of a change in climate, and Senator Goldwater conveniently provided it.

3

THE TROUBLES that have beset the Republican Party in this century took a particularly vexing and mischievous form in 1964. The heart of the problem was that the party simply could not nominate a man whom the majority of the Republicans wanted to see nominated and whom all Republicans could have supported with greater or lesser enthusiasm.

That man might have been Henry Cabot Lodge or it might have been William Scranton or it might have been Richard Nixon, or it might have been someone else, but it certainly was not Barry Goldwater. Goldwater was in truth the minority candidate of the minority party.

When the average was taken of all the contested Republican state primaries of 1964, Senator Goldwater was the choice of no more than one third of the Republican voters. Furthermore, he never had more than a sizable minority in the Harris and Gallup surveys of Republican opinion before the San Francisco convention.

The difficulty in which the Republican party found itself in 1964 seems epitomized in a comment made to me during the campaign by a former Republican national chairman: "Johnson," he said, "was vulnerable this year, and if we could have put up Nixon or Lodge or Scranton or a Rockefeller who had not divorced and remarried, it might have been a different story. If you just look at it that way—Johnson against one of these men—it would have been a horse race. But you can't look at it that way. If the convention had nominated one of them, the conservatives would have walked out. I mean, in the mood they were in at San Francisco, they would have just left the party if Goldwater wasn't nominated, and then where would we have been?"

The roots of this trouble go deep. They stretch back at least to the nomination of Willkie in 1940. At that time the Republican conservatives in and out of Congress were vehemently opposed to the nomination of a liberal "outsider" and renegade Democrat like Willkie. The Taft cause could barely be heard in Philadelphia above the uproar of the "We want Willkie" from galleries packed with a Willkie claque herded into Convention Hall with counterfeit tickets. In their bitter moment of defeat many of the conservatives were convinced under these circumstances that the nomination had been stolen, and this attitude persisted over the years.

"To Taft's people," says his biographer, William S. White, in his book *The Taft Story*, "the Republicans had nominated in Willkie the first of what was to be, in the Taft view, a series of 'me-too' candidates . . . and while a historical process was set on foot that was to alter the whole face of the Republican party and the locus of its ultimate control . . . a personal process set up its work in Taft. This was to increase his suspicion of the 'East,' to make him for years later disinclined to consider Eastern Republicans the genuine article and in general to drive him back upon Middle West associations and attitudes. . . ."

When Roosevelt defeated Willkie to become the first President in history to win a third term, conservative Republicans came to believe that the defeat stemmed from the nomination of a "me-too" candidate who did not offer the voters a true choice between Republicanism and the New Deal. This conviction was intensified when, after having lost to Roosevelt in 1944, Dewey was defeated by Truman in 1948. Taft's reaction was typical. "Here," says White, recalling the Republican loss that year, "was a case where his party—and how he loved it!—had been, as he saw it, let down both by the decision of the Philadelphia convention to run Dewey and then by Dewey's so-called 'me-too' campaign.

"Taft felt to the end that he had been frozen out in the conduct of the campaign, that Governor Dewey was making no real fight against the detested Democrats and that 'Trumanism' or 'New Dealerism' or 'Fair Dealerism'—these were all synonymous to the Senator—had in consequence been fastened upon a suffering country for the foreseeable future. . . .

"He was never reconciled to Dewey's defeat . . . he felt that even if the Republicans had to go down to defeat, they should have gone down in his definition of fighting all the way. What had occurred, as he saw it, was a defeat that was bad enough in itself but intolerable in what seemed to him to have been outright rejection of Republicanism by a Republican candidate."

This feeling among conservative Republicans against leaders of their party who accepted many of the domestic reforms and foreign policy goals of the Democrats was so strong that in announcing its support for Dewey in 1948 the Chicago *Tribune* told its readers, "We consider him the least worse of the candidates."

The conservatives carried their sentiment into the 1952 convention in Chicago, but when the fight was over they accepted Eisenhower, especially after his celebrated Morningside Heights pact with Taft. There was no drastic criticism within the party of Eisenhower's campaign, and his victory brought general rejoicing.

It was only after Eisenhower entered the White House and embarked upon essentially the same course that Roosevelt and Truman had charted that the conservatives began crying "me too" again. By the time he had been in office six months Eisenhower felt so frustrated by the uncooperative antics of the Republican majorities in Congress that he dis-

33

cussed with his colleagues the desirability of trying to start a new third party.

On April 30, 1953, Taft set off a veritable explosion in the Cabinet room after Eisenhower and his fiscal advisers had notified the congressional leaders that the first Republican budget would be out of balance and that the deficits that had made Truman a demon in the eyes of the conservatives would continue for some time. While Eisenhower sat back in astonishment at the outburst, Taft banged his fist on the coffin-shaped Cabinet table and shouted that the efforts of the Eisenhower administration in its first three months had simply produced continued spending on the scale of the Truman administration.

Soon afterward the Republican-controlled Congress proceeded to cut his request for foreign-aid funds and to scale down his housing program. To many Republicans who had sincerely believed that the return of the party to power in 1952 would bring back the good old days of Coolidge and Hoover or maybe even McKinley, Eisenhower seemed like just a typical Democratic President. High taxes continued. Enforcement of the antitrust act went on. Civil rights were extended gradually. Billions of dollars were spent to help foreign countries. The Russians could not be brushed away; they had to be negotiated with just as in the hated days of Roosevelt and Truman. Eisenhower produced the kind of frustration in the right wing that led Senator Joseph R. McCarthy to make a public apology for having supported him for President and caused Senator Goldwater to say that one Eisenhower in a decade was enough.

How strong this feeling among the conservatives was became quite clear with the rise of the Goldwater forces at the Republican National Convention in 1960. Though Vice-President Nixon went to Chicago as the heir apparent to President Eisenhower, he found on his arrival that a boisterous and well-financed movement was under way to win the nomination for Senator Goldwater. Furthermore, the conservatives were furious over the fact that Nixon, in order to avoid a clash with Rockefeller, had gone to the governor's Fifth Avenue apartment in New York City and negotiated an agreement with this kingpin of the Republican liberals on sections of the platform dealing with civil rights, medical care, and national defense. "Sell out on Fifth Avenue!" the Goldwaterites cried.

When Goldwater arrived in Chicago he said that he did not know whether his name would be placed in nomination seriously. The pressure on him to become more than a favorite-son candidate, he conceded, was "very great." Both Arizona, his home state, and South Carolina had instructed their delegations to vote for him.

Despite the rising enthusiasm, Goldwater asked finally that the Arizona delegation refrain from placing his name in nomination. Governor Paul J. Fannin demurred. He delivered a ringing nominating speech for Goldwater explaining to the convention that "This is not an ordinary situation." Seconding speeches were delivered by Representative Bruce Alger of Texas; Gregory D. Shorey, Jr., Republican state chairman of South Carolina; Ray Houck, a South Dakota delegate; and Representative John J. Rhodes of Arizona.

When Goldwater asked to be heard he received an ovation. Loud shouts of "No" rang from the floor when he asked that his name be withdrawn. In words that were to reverberate down to 1964 the senator told the convention that Republicans had been losing elections "not because of too many Democratic votes . . . we have been losing elections because conservatives too often failed to vote. Let's grow up conservatives!" He asked that the delegates supporting him vote for Nixon, but on the one and only roll call he received ten of Louisiana's twenty-six votes. Nixon had won the nomination, but as Robert Novak says in his forthcoming book *The Agony of the GOP 1964,* "The nation suddenly found that a spontaneous mass movement was growing for Goldwater."

Nixon's subsequent defeat by Kennedy released the full energy of this movement. To the increasingly frustrated right wing Nixon had seemed another "me-too" candidate who had thrown away the election by echoing Kennedy and the Democrats in his pursuit of the big-city vote. As never before, a determination was growing among the conservatives that in 1964 the voters were going to be offered the kind of choice that had been denied them for a generation. Combined with this was a resolve by Republicans in the West and South that control of the party must be seized from the East, where it had resided during much of Republican history. McKinley, Taft, Harding, and Hoover had been born in the Midwest, but beginning in 1940 the Republican National Conventions had been dominated by the East. Conservatives who lived beyond the Alleghenies were convinced that if the East were to have its way again in 1964, the party would be stuck with still another losing "me-too" candidate.

Strong new crosscurrents were at work in the party. The East, which used to be the center of Republican reaction, dominated by big business and the trusts, had become the heartland of Republican liberalism. Old wealth, the foundations, the press, the universities, and even the large corporations were moving along modern new paths of political thought. The West, once the backbone of progressivism, was turning conservative under the influence of the nouveaux riches and the fundamentalists immigrating from the Midwest and the South.

Nixon's defeat in 1960 left the West and South in an angry mood of revolt. They wanted to nominate Goldwater in 1964 and take the party on a sharp swerve to the right. Their task was facilitated by the fact that the party had been tending in that direction for several years. The Eisenhower administration had become increasingly, though never radically, conservative during the general's last years in the White House. Eisenhower's tone changed noticeably in his second term. By 1958, after the departure of Sherman Adams, he had dropped his more liberal accents in favor of harsh attacks on the "spenders" in the "radical" wing of the Democratic party in Congress.

At an increasing tempo the party machinery came under conservative and pro-Goldwater influence after 1960. Thus the thirty-five-member Republican Policy Committee in the House was dominated by conservative Midwesterners. The newsletter published by the National Republican Congressional Campaign Committee followed a line that was sometimes to the right of Goldwater. After Representative William E. Miller of New York was elected chairman of the Republican National Committee in 1961, the committee took on more and more of a Goldwater coloration. Some of the higher staff members favored Goldwater so openly that Rockefeller's colleagues protested to national headquarters.

Republicans elected to the House of Representatives in 1960 and 1962 included a number of young conservatives. An idea of how conservative some of them were may be gleaned from their belief that Representative Charles A. Halleck of Indiana, the minority leader, was too much of a liberal. The Young Republicans too played a part in feeding the fervor for Goldwater. It is odd to recall now that in the 1930's the Young Republicans were a liberal crowd whose hero was Harold E. Stassen. As recently as 1949 the Young Republican National Federation met in Salt Lake City and adopted a platform calling for the elimination of the poll tax, antilynching and fair-employment-practices legislation, development of the United Nations "into a world federation," and support of the European recovery program.

The meeting of the federation in San Francisco in 1963, however, was a carnival of extreme conservatism. Donald Lukens of Washington, D.C., was elected president after he had pledged to support Goldwater for the nomination and advocated repeal of the income tax.

Several events in 1962 helped Goldwater's rise. In New York Nelson Rockefeller, up for reelection as governor, needed a huge plurality to demonstrate that he was strong enough to carry the state against the Democrats in 1964. Yet, out of approximately 5,800,000 votes cast, he won by 529,000, which was some 43,000 below his showing in 1958 and a rather lackluster performance in view of Javits' reelection to the Senate at the same time by a 980,000-vote margin.

On the same day, in California, Nixon suffered a calamitous defeat in his ill-advised attempt to win the governorship of California away from Edmund G. (Pat) Brown. Nixon had come within 118,000 votes of winning the Presidency in 1960. He was the titular leader of the party, with great strength still among party workers. Once the effects of 1960 had worn off, he would have been a strong contender for the nomination in 1964. It would have taken patience to wait it out, but Nixon was not patient. Partly because he thought it would improve his chances for another shot at the Presidency, partly to keep the party machinery in California out of the hands of the extreme right, and partly in response to pressure from influential Republicans, especially those who had raised money for him in the past, he entered the California race. The result not only branded him a two-time loser but also provoked him into a tirade against the press that made him look like a poor sport with uncertain control over his own emotions.

Emboldened by these events, some fifty ardent conservative Republicans from all parts of the country met secretly at the Essex Inn in Chicago early in December, 1962, and laid plans to create a National Draft-Goldwater Committee. One of the ringleaders was F. Clifton White, a smooth, able Republican professional from New York who had played a minor role in the 1960 Nixon campaign. From time to time he had met informally with other younger Republicans who were looking for a conservative candidate for 1964. Now they decided to go ahead and start a draft-Goldwater movement and hope that Goldwater would not scuttle it. Placed at its head was Peter O'Donnell, Jr., the youthful Republican state chairman of Texas. O'Donnell formally announced the establishment of the committee at a press conference in Washington on April 8, 1963. In time, state chairmen were appointed in all or most of the states. "I am not taking any position on this draft movement," Goldwater said, and that was all the encouragement the committee needed. Three months later, on the Fourth of July, a large rally was held in Washington.

By this time the popular junior senator from Arizona was the most sought-after speaker in the Republican party. As chairman of the Senate Republican Campaign Committee, he had for years been traveling about the country delivering hundreds of speeches—two hundred and twenty-five in 1961 alone. His political duties took him to large cities and small towns on the prairies; tens of thousands of the party faithful flocked to hear him speak at dinners for which they paid anywhere from five dollars to one thousand dollars a plate. Goldwater came to know a legion of minor party officials. He won the gratitude of hundreds of Republican candidates by making speeches to help them in their campaigns.

Republicans were charmed by his handsome face and sardonic humor. They loved his attacks on the Kennedy administration, the Democratic party, government regulation, high taxes, wasteful spending, and failures in foreign policy. His uncomplicated view of national and international problems made sense to them. His brand of Republicanism appealed to many solid businessmen, doctors, lawyers, farmers, housewives, and students. His heavily ghosted books *The Conscience of a Conservative* and *Why Not Victory?* were bestsellers. Millions of Republicans who were neither "kooks" nor extremists came to admire Goldwater and to believe that he ought to be President. With the possible exception of Nixon, none of the other potential Republican nominees had spent so much time at the grass roots. And far better than his more sophisticated Eastern rivals, Goldwater understood how delegates to the San Francisco convention could be won at the grass roots by the right kind of organization. After all, the majority of the delegates were to be chosen in state conventions. While Rockefeller was setting his sights on the state primaries, which were more dramatic, the Goldwater men were scrounging for delegates precinct by precinct and county by county. They not only wooed the established political leaders but also managed to install hard-core conservative Goldwater supporters in key positions. They worked tirelessly in the states that selected delegates by convention, particularly states in the Rocky Mountains, the Midwest, and the South. By the time Goldwater got to San Francisco he had a powerful base of delegates in the South alone.

In the years leading up to the convention, the conservative movement was dynamic in many parts of the country. The Goldwater cause grew and prospered because his followers were more zealous than other Republicans. In their communities they won control by going to meetings earlier and staying later. In a manner reminiscent of Communist tactics in the labor unions in the 1930's, they infiltrated Republican organizations and won control by outfighting and outlasting their opponents.

"You don't really realize how extreme these people are until you go downstream with them for a while," said a California Republican who was being bucked by militant conservatives trying to capture control in California. Said another, "They follow me around with a goon squad, call me a socialist, and say I must be a Democrat."

Rockefeller's remarriage and the shock of the Negro revolt further tipped the scales toward Goldwater. Indeed, as Novak points out, there was a relation between the two events as far as the Goldwater nomination was concerned. "The impact on Republican Presidential politics of the Negro revolution and the white counterrevolution in May, 1963," he says, "was all the more pronounced because it coincided perfectly with Rockefeller's disastrous marriage. Rockefeller, the Republican party's foremost champion of civil rights, was in decline. Goldwater, the party's national figure most beloved by segregationists, was in ascent."

After the Negro vote helped to elect Kennedy in 1960, the Republican party moved step by step in the direction of the white man's party. Goldwater was convinced that the Negro vote was lost to the Democrats regardless of what the Republicans might do and that the Republicans therefore should seek votes elsewhere.

Goldwater's stand in favor of leaving civil-rights matters to the states was a great asset to him in the South. Then when the racial disorders spread beyond the South, causing considerable fear in the white neighborhoods and suburbs of the North, Goldwater's coolness to federal intervention on behalf of the Negro revolution seemed a potent vote-getting stance in the North as well as in the South. It raised the prospect that he could cater to the Southern white vote, which was regarded as the basis of his Presidential bid, and still win votes of Northerners apprehensive over the advance of the Negroes.

In the end, however, what happened in San Francisco was not so much a matter of Goldwater's winning the nomination as it was of others' losing it. The seizure of power by the extreme conservatives was a revolution in the Republican party all right, and one that followed a familiar pattern. Historically the right wing or the left, as the case may be, comes to power because of weakness at the center. That was the story at San Francisco.

Although Goldwater represented a particular ideology or at least a particular mood, he was not nominated because the party as a whole favored that ideology or shared that mood. All evidence suggests that a majority of the Republicans favored nothing of the sort. Goldwater won because by the time the delegates assembled no one else was strong enough to stop him.

In the four years between the defeat of Nixon in 1960 and

the happenings at the Cow Palace there was adequate power in the Republican party to head off the Goldwater movement. But that power was misused and squandered. If every one of Goldwater's opponents had not done the wrong thing politically, the result would have been different.

All his opponents underestimated the strength of the Goldwater machine. Especially after the senator's poor showing in the early primaries, the moderates deluded themselves into thinking that the convention could not possibly nominate a man whose views, as Karl E. Meyer has written, resembled traditional conservatism about as much as Huey Long's represented traditional liberalism. The Republican liberals were reduced to a gaggle of Micawbers, waiting for something to turn up. Vaguely, that something took the form of General Eisenhower. "Good old Ike will save the party." That was about the size of it.

The truth of the matter was, however, that the former President did not have the inclination, the skill, or indeed the power to name the candidate. It was a game of political infighting, and Eisenhower's influence never lay with the politicians. His influence was with the people, and the people were not much involved in the maneuvering for the Republican nomination.

Furthermore, Eisenhower wanted to stand well with all factions. Goldwater's views did not really keep him awake with worry at night. The former President never wanted to get into the gore of leading one faction against all others. He preferred a role above the battle.

What he did, therefore, was paint himself into a corner. He urged all aspiring Republicans to get into the race. One by one he promised each that he would not back anyone else against him. In the end there was no way for Eisenhower to support any one candidate, even if he had wished to, which, of course, he never did.

At least Eisenhower was consistent to the end. At the time of the governors' conference in Cleveland in June he urged

Scranton not to appear too hard to get if in fact he was willing to accept the nomination. Then, when the headlines suggested that Eisenhower had singled out Scranton as his choice, the former President telephoned Scranton in Cleveland to make sure that Scranton had not mistaken Eisenhower's advice for endorsement. Thereupon Eisenhower was subjected to a good deal of vilification for having pulled the rug from under Scranton. Eisenhower was guilty not of villainy but of causing a great deal of confusion, which was compounded for selfish political reasons by Scranton's staff.

Ultimately the anti-Goldwater movement in the Republican party was doomed for two reasons. One was that until a few weeks before the convention the banner of the other side was in the hands of a man, namely Governor Rockefeller, who suffered a fatal defect in a Presidential aspirant, at least in the year 1964, by virtue of his divorce and remarriage. The other reason was that the many rivals among the moderates and liberals could not, because of temperament or ambition, get together to try to stop Goldwater while there might still have been time.

Scranton could not make up his mind until it was too late. The ablest political professionals in the party offered to work for him six months before the convention, but he told them he did not want to be President. When, after Rockefeller's defeat in the California primary and his own humiliation at the governors' conference, Scranton decided to run, he asked these same professionals to help him, and they said no.

Lodge played it cool in Saigon, where he was the United States ambassador. While hoping for the nomination, he would neither come home and fight for it nor, until it was too late, help someone else defeat Goldwater.

Nixon was the most helpful. He tried to help everyone lose. In that way he could snatch the prize himself. The former Vice-President, who was to call Rockefeller a "party divider" after the Democratic landslide in November, played each contender off against the other. Yet when this proved to be a losing game, he could not bring himself to go it alone for the nomination. The night Goldwater announced that he would vote against cloture in the civil-rights-bill debate or the night he voted against the bill itself—it was one or the other—Nixon telephoned Milton S. Eisenhower at a New York hotel shortly before midnight and said that this was it. The Republican party would go down the drain with an anti-civil-rights candidate, Nixon declared, and so he was going to offer himself as a candidate for the nomination. A splendid idea, Dr. Eisenhower said.

The next thing Dr. Eisenhower knew, however, Nixon had made his way to Washington overnight, hired a limousine, and driven to the general's home at Gettysburg to plead with him to drop his neutrality in view of Goldwater's vote and thereupon call on Republicans to nominate Nixon. Eisenhower did not do so, and Nixon did not throw his own hat in the ring.

As late as June 2 Goldwater might have been sidetracked from the nomination if Rockefeller had defeated him in the California primary. But almost on the eve of the primary all the other moderates, still hoping for the nomination even though they were not running in the primary, issued disclaimers that a vote for Rockefeller would be a vote for their cause. And General Eisenhower said that a statement he had issued on his ideal for a candidate was not aimed at Goldwater, even though everyone else under the sun read it that way. Thus Goldwater squeezed through with fifty-one percent of the vote.

It was a year when a moderate Republican might have run a strong race against President Johnson, but after California the Republican party was in the grip of forces that made the nomination of such a candidate impossible.

4

Barry Goldwater entered the campaign with certain built-in handicaps, and he made the most of them.

There is simply no substantial body of opinion anywhere in either party or outside the parties that holds that the Republican Presidential campaign of 1964 was shrewd, effective, or inspiring. Numerous issues existed that a Republican candidate could have exploited against President Johnson, and Goldwater touched upon many of them.

The drawback was that the Goldwater who emerged as a Presidential candidate was unacceptable to a large majority of the voters, including millions of Republicans. The Goldwater candidacy itself nullified the force of these other issues. It did little good, for example, for Goldwater to criticize the conduct of the war in Southeast Asia when, as the election returns showed, a majority of the voters would not dream of letting him take charge of such a dangerous situation. All questions therefore became subordinate to the question of Goldwater's fitness for the Presidency.

To be sure 1964 was a year when no Republican could have run with high hope of winning. The country was enormously prosperous. Employment was high. The stock market was steady and prices fairly stable. The business forecast was generally favorable. The days when many voters instinctively identified the Republicans as the party of good times were long past.

Outside the entanglement in South Vietnam, the country

was at peace, or as much so at least as the people had come to know in the Cold War era. Even the American casualties in Vietnam were too few and too scattered to arouse public opinion.

Johnson had taken office on November 22, 1963, under circumstances bound to bring him maximum sympathy and goodwill. He then made an excellent impression with the skill, generally acknowledged on all sides, with which he managed the transition between administrations. President Kennedy had left him a generous legacy in the civil-rights bill and the tax bill, both of which Johnson dexterously guided through Congress. Moreover, the tragedy at Dallas made John Fitzgerald Kennedy a poignant and legendary figure in American history, whose memory enhanced the Democratic party in a way certain to attract votes in states like Massachusetts, New York, California, Illinois, Pennsylvania, Michigan, and others.

Another factor working in Johnson's favor was the custom of the American people, particularly strong in this country, of electing a President to a second term unless some extraordinary event intervenes. Only twice since 1900 have Presidents been defeated when running for a second term—Taft in 1912, when the Bull Moose split the Republican party, and Hoover in 1932, when the country was gripped by the Depression. A Goldwater victory in 1964 would have given the United States a third President in little more than a year's time, which would have been a radical departure from previous experience.

From the time his candidacy was conceived, during the Kennedy administration, the Goldwater strategy was predicated on carrying the South, which was thought to be ready to revolt against the Kennedy brothers and their civil-rights policies. The assassination impaired this strategy by installing a Southerner in the White House for the first time (excepting Woodrow Wilson, who was born in Virginia but was reared in the North) in almost one hundred years.

Finally, Senator Goldwater was pitted against a party that had been in the majority for a generation and against a candidate who was campaigning from the White House with its incomparable forum and its levers for manipulating support from all sorts of groups and interests. From the very beginning the President looked like the probable winner, giving him an aura that Goldwater only enhanced by his interview with the German magazine *Der Spiegel* before the Republican National Convention. He said that as of then he could not, if nominated, defeat Johnson, but felt he could make a "different horse race" of it by November. Instead the public opinion polls invariably showed Goldwater to be trailing far behind the President. His entire campaign therefore had the smell of defeat about it throughout.

It is nearly inconceivable that any Republican could have surmounted these handicaps. But certainly the party could have done better, and in doing so would have built a much stronger base on which it could now prepare for the future. Recounting the mistakes of the Goldwater campaign is a futile exercise, but it does point the way around pitfalls that still lie ahead. The Republican party can scarcely take another 1964.

The errors fell into six broad categories:

1. Senator Goldwater frightened away large numbers of voters by giving the impression that he would make a sharp break with the past at a time when the country was in no mood for radical change.

2. With a folly whose dimensions can be grasped only in the fullness of time, he drove practically the entire Negro vote in the United States into the Democratic party, whence it will not soon be dislodged.

3. The senator belligerently refused to conciliate the various factions of his own party to achieve a unified campaign.

4. With a couple of inconspicuous exceptions, he offered the voters no concrete, constructive programs.

5. He isolated himself from the people.

6. With careless use of words and ideas, he aroused fear that he might get the country into war.

From the outset of his quest for the Presidency Goldwater filled the political woods with hobgoblins of changes in the American way of life, changes that he probably could not or would not have made had he been elected. Ideas he had been tossing off blithely on the banquet circuit for years sounded altogether different and more frightening on the lips of a man running for the Presidency.

Large numbers of elderly voters all over the country were alienated by his offhand suggestion in the New Hampshire primary campaign that Social Security might be placed on a voluntary basis. When President Johnson carried Florida in the election, he ran best in the Miami and St. Petersburg-Tampa areas, where many retired men and women live on their Social Security checks.

In the region of the Tennessee Valley Authority the Republican nominee obviously lost votes by his suggestion months earlier that the government sell the TVA. In the farm states voters were fearful that Goldwater would abolish price supports and cut back the Rural Electrification Administration. That was one reason for his surprisingly bad showing in the rural Midwest.

In the middle of the campaign he made a speech in Knoxville, in the heart of the TVA country, saying he stood by all he had said about the "socialistic" TVA. By way of trying to paper over a damaging issue, he added that the TVA was a creature of Congress and that if he became President he could not sell it if he wished to unless Congress approved. He took the same line with farmers in discussing price supports.

The trouble with this approach was that it made it appear that he would be a weak President who might want to do away with things like the TVA and price supports but would be prevented by a Congress looking out for the people's interests. His various statements favoring the "dilution" of Presidential powers added to this effect.

During the 1948 campaign political analyst Samuel Lubell made the rather surprising discovery that to many of the voters "Truman rather than Dewey seemed the conservative candidate." If that was true in 1948, it was true one hundred times over in the 1964 campaign, when millions of voters regarded Johnson as a middle-of-the-road conservative and Goldwater as a radical or extremist who might make unpredictable changes in American society.

Throughout the campaign Goldwater, the candidate of the party of Lincoln, made no gestures worthy of the name to the Negro people, no appeal of any consequence to the Negro vote.

The race riots in the spring of 1964 made the Goldwater strategists more certain than ever that a white "backlash" was building up in the North that was capable of providing enough of a "silent vote" to elect the Republican candidate. The heavy vote received by Alabama's Governor George C. Wallace in the Indiana, Wisconsin, and Maryland primaries contributed to this belief. The concentration in Goldwater's early campaign speeches on lawlessness, violence, and disorder in the streets was beamed directly at this supposed vote of white protest.

Goldwater had antagonized all Negroes by voting against the civil-rights bill in the Senate. He worsened his case in their eyes by saying in a campaign speech in Minneapolis in September: "I charge with a sincerely heavy heart that the more the federal government has attempted to legislate morality the more it has incited hatred and violence."

By repute Senator Goldwater was not a segregationist, but the Negroes were never under any illusions about the support given him by racists everywhere. Their reaction was caught in the words of Louis Lomax, author of *The Negro Revolt*, when he wrote during the campaign: "Goldwater had the support of known anti-Negro elements in

49

local communities across the nation. It became equally clear that he welcomed, rather than denied, their support. And it was this, the nature of the local elements supporting Goldwater, that turned the Negro anti-Goldwater tide into a raging flood."

In September Goldwater did what no other Presidential candidate would have dreamed of doing when he went through the South denouncing the Supreme Court and preaching states' rights. In the South, of course, the phrase "states' rights" includes among other things the connotation of local management of the racial problem. He never once mentioned civil rights.

No previous Presidential candidate in modern times had dared put on such a performance. Throughout the postwar years Eisenhower, Nixon, Kennedy, Johnson, and Adlai E. Stevenson, each in his day, said in the South what was generally accepted as the right thing to say about civil rights. Sometimes forthrightly, sometimes gingerly, always tactfully, they took a stand in the South in favor of an end to discrimination based on race, color, or creed. What they were doing really was saying in the South things that would demonstrate to the rest of the country that they were on the right side of the civil-rights issue. They were willing to risk votes in the South to win a greater number of votes in the North. Goldwater went straight for the white Southern vote without a care, evidently, about how his words would sound elsewhere.

At no time during his Southern tour was any effort made to conceal the lily-white nature of the Goldwater campaign. On the contrary, it was emphasized by such theatrical effects as the appearance of seven hundred Alabama girls in long white gowns at Goldwater's speech in Montgomery's Crampton Bowl and by the ritual of Strom Thurmond's switch from the Democratic to the Republican party in South Carolina. Thurmond, the most candid racist in the United States Senate, was embraced by Goldwater and held up by him as a shining example to all Democrats in the South. Nothing about the Southern trip was more arresting than the almost total absence of Negroes in the crowds wherever Goldwater went. Richard Rovere observed in *The New Yorker* that probably no one before had "ever logged several thousand miles in the South and visited a dozen or so of its great centers of population without seeing any more Negroes than one might expect to encounter on, say, an average winter afternoon in Spitsbergen."

The consequences of Goldwater's utter indifference to the Negro vote were revealed in the election returns. The Republican party won Alabama, Mississippi, South Carolina, and Louisiana, but it lost Virginia, Tennessee, and Florida, which had gone for Nixon in 1960. The Negro vote was an important factor in the change. In the country at large it helped Johnson greatly. An estimated ninety-five percent of all Negro voters voted Democratic. In some districts the total fell just short of one hundred percent.

The Republicans not only lost the largest single racial voting bloc in the country but also saw the supposed "backlash" vote vanish into thin air. There was no backlash to speak of, owing in large part no doubt to the moratorium on racial demonstrations. Even areas that had voted for Wallace in the primaries went heavily for Johnson. The Goldwater strategists who thought that resentment against Negro gains in the South and in the North could send the Democrats to defeat were dead wrong. The Republican party paid a dear price for their error.

As if Goldwater did not have enough disadvantages to contend with, he resolutely started out on the wrong foot the day after he was nominated. The San Francisco convention had been one of the bitterest in the party's history. Respected leaders had been jeered. Party traditions had been severely wrenched. A new crowd with ideas foreign to many Republicans had forced its way to power. Many individuals were left with hurt feelings and wounded pride.

Not least among the moderates' irritations was Goldwater's designation of Representative William E. Miller of New York as his running mate. Aside from a short and unhappy term as chairman of the Republican National Committee, Miller had achieved no national reputation; if he was known at all, people remembered him vaguely as a former district attorney from a rural county in upstate New York. After the tragic events in Dallas in November, 1963, the Vice-Presidency could no longer be viewed merely as part of the patronage of the Presidential nominee. Goldwater's choice of Miller only emphasized the repudiation of the moderates that characterized the convention.

That time of soreness and raw nerves that often follows the balloting had come over the convention when, on the final night, Goldwater arrived to deliver his acceptance speech. This was the hour, familiar in the history of conventions, when the health of the party, so necessary in the campaign ahead, was waiting to be restored by conciliation on the part of the winners toward the losers. It was the moment when tradition required that the winner extend the olive branch, enabling his opponents to swallow old animosities and join him in seeking victory for the sake of the party.

Desperately as he was to need this help, Barry Goldwater held out no olive branch. "Anyone who joins us in all sincerity we welcome," he said. "Those who do not care for our cause we don't expect to enter our ranks in any case." In the heat of battle his opponents had said that he was an extremist, and now before a huge national television audience he threw it back in their faces. He even underlined the words in his text: "I would remind you that extremism in defense of liberty is no vice. And let me remind you also that moderation in the pursuit of justice is no virtue!"

Politics is controlled by events, not by words, but the San Francisco acceptance speech was an event. It was an arrogant blunder that hardened the division between the two wings of the party, closed the convention in disharmony in-

52

stead of conciliation, and gave a certain tone to the Goldwater campaign that never entirely died away.

The speech almost carried the Republican party to the breaking point.

The text was drafted by Karl Hess, a hard-line conservative, who was the senator's principal speech writer; it was approved by a dozen top members of Goldwater's staff at the Mark Hopkins Hotel. Whatever Hess, the staff, and the candidate may have intended to convey, the words, spoken against the background of that time of racial discord, sounded ominous to Negroes and other minority groups, who had the most reason to fear extremism. It was a time, after all, when the Ku Klux Klan was riding to the defense of liberty as the Klan understood liberty. Perhaps this was why the speech was so enthusiastically received in some parts of the South. For this same reason, naturally, Republican leaders of the North found it difficult to live with. The first to attack it was Governor Rockefeller, who called it "dangerous, irresponsible, and frightening."

Goldwater's seeming defense of extremism made it just that much more impossible for Republicans like Keating, Romney, and Lindsay to endorse him or for those like Scott, Percy, Taft, Governor James A. Rhodes of Ohio, and many others to give him anything but the scantest recognition.

Whereas Eisenhower had compromised with Taft on Morningside Heights and Nixon had compromised with Rockefeller on Fifth Avenue, Goldwater had delivered an uncompromising acceptance speech, after which he and his associates proceeded to rip the staff of the Republican National Committee to pieces to make sure that few were left who would have been discomfited by the tone of his remarks in San Francisco.

Like so many other things Goldwater was to do in the campaign, the speech played into Johnson's hands by making him appear to be the safer candidate, the man in the middle of the road, the one who would be President of all the people, who was moderate and conciliatory, who would unify the nation, heal its wounds, and not inflame an already dangerous situation created by the race riots.

From the Goldwater point of view there was also another unfortunate consequence, which was to recur time and again after other speeches. This was that once the full adverse affect of his words upon the country became evident he had to start talking himself out of them. Thus even before Senator Goldwater departed from San Francisco, General Eisenhower became upset over the remarks about extremism. To reassure him Goldwater told the general, "The most extreme action that you can take in the defense of freedom is to go to war. When you led those troops across the channel into Normandy, you were being an extremist."

Some of his clarifications of other speeches and remarks were equally ludicrous. When, for example, his statement that the Democrats were "soft on Communism" backfired because of the widespread disapproval of this return to the idiom of the McCarthy era, Goldwater explained that Richard Nixon and Herbert Hoover suggested that he say it.

The worst of it was not that the explanations did or did not explain but that they served to keep alive subjects that the senator might better have avoided in the first place. Among these, even more harmful to Goldwater than the epigram about extremism, was an endless string of speeches, statements, and off-the-cuff remarks about nuclear weapons.

It is a perfectly valid question whether, as Goldwater proposed, the supreme commander of NATO should be authorized in advance of certain contingencies to use nuclear weapons under carefully delineated conditions. But this is a peculiarly difficult and delicate subject to debate in a heated Presidential election campaign. General Eisenhower, who was unusually well qualified to understand it, was preeminent among those who thought the issue was not one to be batted about at the whistle-stops. Where Senator Goldwater expected to win any votes on this question is hard to imagine. Yet it should not have been hard to foresee—as many of his unhappy staff apparently did foresee—what pitfalls lay ahead once he got into it.

Before the campaign began there had been a rather long history of disconnected and blunt remarks by Goldwater concerning nuclear weapons and showdowns with Communist nations, which made a risky political background for the senator's campaign proposals on tactical-nuclear-weapons control. It was not entirely reassuring to a great many citizens that he had voted against ratification of the nuclear-test-ban treaty. But in addition to that he had had so much to say about brinkmanship, letting military commanders do the job, sending Marines to turn the water on at Guantánamo, knocking down the Berlin wall, the superiority of America's nuclear weapons, the weakness of Russia, the vulnerability of Cuba, and the necessity of being prepared for military operations against vulnerable Communist regimes that he all too often sounded predisposed to military venturing. Henry Brandon, the Washington correspondent of the London *Sunday Times,* reported that in the senator's campaign speech at Hammond, Indiana, "I heard him mention the words 'war,' 'nuclear weapons,' 'holocaust,' and 'destruction' twenty-five times in about as many minutes."

The most damaging and perhaps the most unfairly reported of Goldwater's military statements was his discussion on a television program of the possibility of nuclear "defoliation" of the South Asian jungles.

The rat-a-tat-tat of Goldwater's comments on the bomb and foreign policy raised serious questions as to whether the senator was speaking from any great depth of knowledge and reflection on these problems. It did more than that. It enabled the Democrats with a little distortion here and a little exaggeration there to create in the minds of millions of voters an image of Goldwater as a reckless, "trigger-happy" man who might well get the country into war by design or by blunder. The more Goldwater kept talking about nuclear weapons and issuing clarifications of previous statements, the more he served to color the image.

Without doubt the fear that a Goldwater administration might somehow lead to war was the most powerful single factor Johnson had on his side. Everywhere reporters and poll takers found voters worried about what Goldwater would do abroad. This was especially true in the suburbs, where parents worried about their children's living close to prospective target areas in time of war. This worry was undoubtedly the main reason why many men and women who might otherwise have been expected to vote Republican deserted Goldwater. Bobby Baker, Walter Jenkins, Billie Sol Estes, the stereo set, and all the rest of the Goldwater nuggets seemed inconsequential alongside questions of war and peace.

Imprudent and imprecise utterances on military policy and nuclear weapons, extending back over a long period, proved costly to Goldwater in 1964. A more cautious man seeking the Presidency would have avoided many of the traps that snared Senator Goldwater. Even well-informed persons who were not taken in by innuendoes that Goldwater was itching to drop the bomb were fearful that his foreign policy might lead in the end to an ultimatum to the Soviet Union and thus produce the same result. The mere fact that he was forced to declare that he did not favor going to war put him in somewhat the 1940 position of Willkie, who found it necessary to insist that he had never had an office on Wall Street. The mere idea was enough to do the damage.

Goldwater never really offered a consistent, convincing, reassuring exposition of what his foreign policy would be. He made it clear that he intended to be tougher toward the Russians and the Cubans. In fact, he proposed to treat all Communist regimes with equal and uncompromising hostility, a policy, incidentally, that none of this country's allies would support. Goldwater promised to strengthen the

56

NATO alliance, yet it was plain that the policies he proposed were abhorrent to all the NATO allies. He was critical of nearly every step taken by Kennedy and Johnson to advance the cause of peaceful coexistence with the Soviet Union.

In domestic policy the Goldwater of 1964 was like the socialists of the 1930's in the sense that he had a philosophy of sorts but no real program for putting it into effect. When he made his farm speech at the National Plowing Contest at Buffalo, North Dakota, he broke with tradition and offered no farm program. In fact he insisted that the complexities of farm legislation were not his specialty. To be sure, he was against the Democratic bureaucracy, but he had "no intention of dropping supports overnight." The senator offered no comprehensive programs in the fields of conservation, civil rights, housing, abolition of poverty, education, housing, and modernization of the teeming cities.

In retrospect only two specific new domestic proposals come to mind from his campaign speeches. One was a plan for a twenty-five-percent income-tax cut in five annual five-percent installments. This proposal was a trifle suspect in view of the fact that he had voted against the eleven-billion-dollar tax cut in the 1964 Congress. In addition, his stand on military policy seemed to call for even greater rather than smaller outlays. The other proposal was a plan for returning part of the federal revenues to the states. He broached it and then let it slide, and the next thing that was heard on the subject was that President Johnson put it forward as a major program of his own.

Gimmicks became substitutes for issues of public policy in the Goldwater campaign. A Goldwater front organization, Mothers for Moral America, sponsored a movie called *Choice*, which was supposed to show how wicked things had become under the Democrats but was itself of such dubious propriety that Goldwater ordered it canceled. Though there were the most searching criticisms to be made of the administration's defense policies, they were lost in the giggles over the senator's attack on "Yo-Yo" McNamara. Goldwater did hit upon the idea of dispatching Eisenhower to South Vietnam if he were elected. On learning of the project after the senator had mentioned it, however, Eisenhower was anything but receptive. Following the Jenkins affair Goldwater centered his campaign on the issue of immorality, broadly defined. In view of the downward trend of moral standards throughout the world since World War II, if not indeed since World War I, it was a dubious burden to place upon a President who had been in office only eleven months.

One of the things about the Goldwater campaign that was hardest to understand was the candidate's avoidance of crowds and excitement. It was ironical that the peculiar contribution to political lore by the man who had one of the most fervent followings in history should have been that he conducted the most undemonstrative campaign in history.

With one exception, and that a slipup apparently, he held no press conferences during the campaign. When he visited the cities he generally avoided the crowds, the slums, and the ghettos and appeared only in halls filled with militant conservatives who needed no persuasion by him. There was precious little effort on the senator's part to take his case to the unconvinced.

Anyone who had lived through Harry Truman's "give-'em-hell" campaign had to wonder at the comparison Goldwater's followers tried to draw between the plight of their candidate at the end of October, 1964, and the predicament of Mr. Truman at the end of October, 1948. Both were trailing in the polls, it is true, but the comparison ended there.

Where Goldwater was plodding, Harry Truman had been blazing. His train was his trademark, and he was fighting from the canyons of New York to the canyons of Colorado. He was like an underdog in the last round, standing in the ring slugging it out toe-to-toe with the champion until the crowd was hysterical. Truman was all gusto, all movement, all guts, all bravado. No one who knew anything about American politics could have compared the climax of his campaign with that of Goldwater's. While Goldwater to the end addressed the faithful, Truman talked to those with the votes. To the Negroes he promised civil rights. Before labor he denounced the Taft-Hartley law as the "slave-labor act." To the city dwellers he pledged housing. To the farmers he offered subsidies. To the West he held out the vision of water. The comparison between Truman and Goldwater at the end of their respective campaigns calls to mind Henry L. Mencken's comment in 1948. "What had Dewey to offer against all this pie-in-the-sky?" he asked. "Virtually nothing." A rather good, short, recent history of the Republican party.

Goldwater's campaign was remarkably stern and cheerless. Apart from some humor no deeper than wisecracks, it wore a long face. Under Johnson the corn market broke all records, but at least his campaign had some warmth about it.

In all probability the most serious flaw in the Goldwater campaign was that the candidate lost sight of the thing that had put him in the Presidential picture in the first place—his special philosophy of conservatism. Instead of trying to persuade the American people to vote for conservative principles he was all over the lot with Billie Sol Estes, "Yo-Yo" McNamara, Strom Thurmond, TVA, control of tactical nuclear weapons, and condemnation of pornography. The issue of conservatism versus liberalism became lost in the rush.

"The Great Debate did not take place," Henry Brandon lamented, "and so a historic opportunity was missed. But why? There is no simple answer. The most obvious explanation is that Senator Goldwater did not have the capabilities and the equipment to mount and sustain this debate."

5

OF ALL THE WRONG GUESSES that went into the Republican Presidential nomination of 1964, the most spectacularly wrong was the guess that hordes of voters who had stayed home when "me-too" candidates had run would come swarming to the polls to elect a right-wing Republican like Barry Goldwater.

Of all the lessons the election returns taught, the clearest is that the Republican party, if it is ever to win again, must nominate a candidate who can attract the votes of Democrats and independents as well as Republicans.

The Republicans who conceived and accomplished the nomination of Senator Goldwater were the prisoners of their own myth, one of rather old vintage at that. The supposed untapped reservoir of conservative votes, now proved to be a mirage, was envisi ed by Robert A. Taft and his followers in the frusu tion over the defeats of Willkie and Dewey.

Like Goldwater, the Taft wing believed that the Republican party was losing Presidential elections because it was not nominating candidates who could bring out a decisive but petulantly stay-at-home conservative vote. In his speech to the Republican National Convention in 1960, it will be recalled, Goldwater said that "We have been losing elections because the conservatives too often fail to vote." In fact, on November 3, 1964, the percentage of eligible voters who cast ballots was actually *lower* than in 1960 (although the number of voters in 1964, 69,306,122, was higher than in 1960). Far from bringing out a hypothetical silent vote, the Goldwater-Johnson campaign attracted proportionately fewer votes than did the Nixon-Kennedy contest.

After Kennedy defeated Nixon, Goldwater was asked in an interview why he thought the Republicans had lost. "My explanation," he replied, "is that the Republicans, frankly, ran a 'me-too' candidate. And once again, as in 1940, 1944, and 1948, we tried to outpromise the Democrats. I'm convinced it can't be done."

"Where does the Republican party go from here?" he was asked.

"I believe," he replied, "the Republican party should have learned its lesson—that it must be a conservative party. The next election should be contested by conservatives, not by people who ape the New Deal."

The very day after Nixon lost, Goldwater attributed his defeat to "a repeat performance of 1944 and 1948, when we offered the voters insufficient choice with a 'me-too' candidate." Goldwater could scarcely have dreamed then that when he came to offer the voters a sufficient choice in 1964 he would receive eight million fewer votes than were cast for Nixon in 1960.

What is even more incredible is that only a matter of days before Goldwater was to lose to Johnson by the greatest plurality in history, certain eminent members of his staff believed that the "silent" conservative vote was going to save him. Amazing though it sounds today, it may be said on reliable authority that shortly before the election, when the public-opinion polls showed Johnson leading by more than sixty to forty, a high Republican campaign strategist, ruminating on the silent vote, expressed concern that Goldwater was "peaking"—reaching the climax of his campaign—too soon.

Over the years the cry that only a dyed-in-the-wool conservative could win was both a means of disguising the real reasons for Republican losses and of creating sentiment for the nomination of the kind of candidate the conservatives wanted.

Goldwater's campaign had scarcely begun when the claim about the hidden reservoir of Republican strength began to evaporate. In September, 1964, a large number of leading business executives, most of them Republicans and many of them prominent members of the Eisenhower administration, announced their support of the Johnson-Humphrey ticket. Not since the New Deal alienated the business community thirty years ago had big business and big finance supported a Democratic nominee on anything like the scale of support given Johnson. Obviously the reason these Republican businessmen backed the President was not that they had become converts to the Democratic party but that they distrusted Goldwater's brand of right-wing conservatism. Thus in an area of massive Republican strength in the past, the nomination of Goldwater seriously weakened the party. Nixon's comment that same month that "the Democratic party is now the party of big business" cannot seem very funny to Republicans today.

Another area of past Republican strength that was sapped by Goldwater's type of conservatism was the support of a large and influential segment of the press. The Republican press turned in large part to the support of Johnson. This shift was due primarily to the fact that the owners and editors of these papers doubted Goldwater's policies and qualifications. But it undoubtedly indicated also that in many of the cities represented by these papers the banking, business, and financial communities were agreeable to going along with another term for Johnson in view of the Goldwater candidacy.

It is safe to assume that if there were a large, decisive bloc of conservative votes lying in wait for a conservative, Republicans like Rockefeller, Keating, Romney, Scott, Percy, and Taft would have been loath either to turn their backs on the national ticket or merely to give it lip service. Instead of bringing out the hidden votes of conservatives, the Goldwater nomination tore the Republican party apart the way the Democratic party was torn apart when the Free Silver Democrats captured the convention of 1896 and nominated William Jennings Bryan. Just as Bryan's radicalism on money, banks, and trusts drove moderate Democrats to the support of McKinley, Goldwater's extreme, if not radical, positions on a great many issues drove moderate Republicans to the support of Johnson.

The forces who got the upper hand at San Francisco and nominated Goldwater so greatly exaggerated the potential conservative vote that they overlooked the broad progressive strain that runs through the Republican party in spite of its essentially conservative coloration. Republican progressivism did not end with Theodore Roosevelt. As Walter Lippmann recently reminded us, Hoover in his own troubled administration adopted virtually all the main principles that were later embodied in the New Deal.

"It was Mr. Hoover," Lippmann wrote, "who abandoned the principles of *laissez faire* in relation to the business cycle, established the conviction that prosperity and depression can be publicly controlled by political action, and drove out of the public consciousness the old idea that depressions must be overcome by private adjustment."

Lippmann recalled that Hoover in his acceptance speech in 1932 held that "the function of the federal government in these times is to use its reserve powers and its strength for the protection of citizens and local governments by support to our institutions against forces beyond their control."

"Hoover's recovery program," Lippmann added, "included a deliberate policy of inflating the base of credit, reduction of the normal expenses of government, but an increase of extraordinary expenditures—the expansion of public works in order to create employment, the assumption by the federal government of the ultimate responsibility for relief of destitution where local or private resources were inadequate. This increase was not to be covered by taxation but by deficit financing."

The Federal Farm Board and the Reconstruction Finance Corporation, both established by the Hoover administration, were the forerunners of the New Deal spending agencies.

The late Senator Arthur H. Vandenberg, Republican, of Michigan, not only fathered the Federal Deposit Insurance act of the 1930's, but later, as chairman of the Senate Foreign Relations Committee, was indispensable to the passage of the Marshall Plan and the ratification of the North Atlantic Treaty.

However much he may have grumbled about the "creeping socialism" of the TVA, President Eisenhower accepted the basic reforms of the New Deal and in fact broadened some of them. Nixon, if he had been elected, would undoubtedly have been more progressive, particularly in such areas as civil rights and medical care for the elderly. Charles Halleck and Representative William M. McCulloch, Republican, of Ohio, made it possible in October, 1963, for President Kennedy to get the civil-rights bill through the House Judiciary Committee. Republican governors past and present like Earl Warren in California, Dewey and Rockefeller in New York, Youngdahl in Minnesota, Scranton in Pennsylvania, Herter in Massachusetts, Romney in Michigan, and Carlson in Kansas have provided progressive administrations.

In recent years the majority of Republicans in Congress voted for the civil-rights bill, the nuclear-test-ban treaty, the tax cut, the United States Arms Control and Disarmament Agency, the national-defense-education act, the UN loan, and the trade-expansion act.

In the spring of 1964 the Republican Critical Issues Council, which was headed by Milton S. Eisenhower and which represented a rather broad spectrum of opinion within the party, issued a series of papers that were in the progressive

Republican tradition. In the field of civil rights, for example, the council recommended both federal fair-employment-practices legislation and legislation guaranteeing Negroes the right to public accommodations. These were the very provisions of the civil-rights bill upon which Goldwater based his negative vote on the grounds that both were unconstitutional.

Although the New Hampshire Presidential primary last March proved to have no important bearing on the outcome of the convention, the results told something about the mood of Republican voters. Here was an old-line Republican state with a basically conservative, educated electorate. Yet in a field that included Lodge, Rockefeller, Nixon, Margaret Chase Smith, and Stassen, Goldwater received only twenty-three percent of the votes. New Hampshire, though only a small sampling, made it fairly obvious that Goldwater, if nominated, would not run well even among Republicans.

Of course it is true that about one third of all the adults in the United States do not vote in Presidential elections. A sizable proportion of these are ineligible for technical reasons, such as being unable to pass literacy tests, to meet current residence requirements, and so forth. The rest of the nonvoters are made up very largely of persons at the lower end of the economic scale.

In a recent study of nonvoters Gallup arrived at a statistical picture of the eligible voters least likely to vote. This person is a woman in her twenties who has had little formal education and is married to a manual laborer. It is perfectly absurd to suppose that this is the kind of citizen who has been staying away from the polls waiting for a conservative Republican candidate to turn up. On the contrary, she is almost certainly a "pocketbook-issue" voter who, if she went to the polls at all, would cast her ballot for the Democrats.

Historically the percentage of Republicans who vote is larger than the percentage of Democrats who vote. It is apparent, therefore, that the Republicans would find it harder than the Democrats to uncover an untapped source of voters. According to Gallup, nine million Republicans did not vote in 1960. But the number of persons classifying themselves as Democrats who stayed home was eighteen million, many of them poor Negroes in the South. There seems to be a basis, therefore, for Democratic claims that it is they who would gain if all those eligible to vote went to the polls.

Before the San Francisco convention Gallup made a survey to get a picture of the relative numerical strength of the conservatives and the liberals, or moderates, in the Republican party. Dividing Nixon's strength equally between the two wings because of uncertainty as to which the former Vice-President should be identified with, the study showed a division of fifty-five percent liberals and thirty percent conservatives.

Only in the Deep South did a large number of conservative votes turn up in the Republican column in the 1964 election for the first time, and they were cast primarily in protest against the Democratic administration's stand on civil rights. Except for the favorite-son vote in Arizona, the rest of the country—even the Rocky Mountain states, once called "Goldwater country"—voted overwhelmingly against the conservative Republican nominee.

Johnson carried scores of counties that had not voted for a Democratic Presidential candidate since World War I or earlier. Conservative New England Yankees wanted no part of Goldwater's conservatism. Even Boston's Beacon Hill went Democratic. Johnson swept more than three hundred and fifty New England towns that the Republicans had held even in the 1936 Roosevelt landslide. It is clear that Goldwater lost the Northeast after his primary campaign in New Hampshire, where he established himself in the minds of many voters as a radical on issues like the United Nations, Social Security, and the use of nuclear weapons. Speeches he made in New Hampshire also were heard on radio and television in Maine and Vermont. On election day more than six out of every ten voters in Vermont and seven out of ten in Maine cast their votes for Lyndon Johnson. Upstate New York counties, where one's social standing was once impaired by saying a good word for F.D.R., went solidly Democratic. Westchester County, pleasant domain of the lordliest Republicans, voted Democratic for the first time in half a century.

The fate of Goldwater's conservatism in Ohio brings to mind the reminiscences of the late Brand Whitlock, author and diplomat, about the Ohio of his youth. "The Republican party was not a faction, not a group, not a wing, it was an institution like those Emerson speaks of in his essay on Politics, rooted like oak trees in the center around which men group themselves as best they can. It was a fundamental and self-evident thing, like life and liberty, and the pursuit of happiness, or like the flag or the federal judiciary. It was elemental like gravity, the sun, the stars, the ocean. It was merely a synonym for patriotism, another name for the nation. One became, in Urbana and in Ohio for many years, a Republican just as the Eskimo dons fur clothes. It was inconceivable that any self-respecting man should be a Democrat." It was in a state with a heritage like this that there should have been, if it existed anywhere, a troop of stout conservatives ready to redeem the past if offered a candidate like Goldwater. But Johnson carried Ohio by more than one million votes.

Even when the anti-Goldwater tide dragged down local Republican candidates, many of these losers received more votes than Goldwater. This was true, for example, in the cases of Robert A. Taft, Jr., who ran for United States senator in Ohio; Senator Kenneth B. Keating in New York; Charles H. Percy, who ran for governor of Illinois; Senator J. Glenn Beall in Maryland; and John Davis Lodge, who ran for senator in Connecticut.

In other notable cases Republicans who shunned Goldwater's doctrines were elected. Governor Romney won in Michigan. State Representative Daniel Jackson Evans was elected governor of Washington. Senator Hugh Scott was reelected in Pennsylvania. And Representative Lindsay was sent back to Washington by New York City's seventeenth ("Silk Stocking") Republican district.

The conservative tide failed to surge in to keep afloat many of the most rock-ribbed conservatives in Congress. Thus Representative Katharine St. George of New York lost her Rockland County seat by 5,414 votes. Representative Steven B. Derounian, also of New York, lost his Nassau County seat by 3,222. Representative John R. Pillion of New York lost his seat in Tully by 14,511. Representative R. Walter Riehlman of New York lost his seat in Rochester by 4,514. In Ohio Representative Carl W. Rich lost by 5,270. In Michigan Representative George Meader of Grosse Point lost by 1,742 and Representative August E. Johansen by 5,320. In Pennsylvania Representative James D. Weaver lost by 4,550. In Colorado Representative J. Edgar Chenoweth lost by 6,848. In Maine a Republican candidate for Congress, Kenneth P. MacLeod, lost by 41,826. And the list could be extended.

Commenting on the election returns, Nixon said that the party "went too far to the right." Yet not even a landslide seemed to rid the extreme right of its convictions that the authentic road to defeat was the nomination of a "me-too" candidate.

At his press conference in the Camelback Inn in Scottsdale, Arizona, the day after the election, Goldwater regretted that "the more liberal, or moderate, members of the Republican party" had sat on their hands during the campaign.

"I think they are entitled to do what they want," he said, "but I don't think we can build a Republican party on their concepts, which in my opinion have no difference at all with the Democratic concepts."

In fact the right wing seemed not to have learned any lesson at all from the defeat.

"One year's landslide loss, in other words," wrote William F. Buckley, Jr., editor in chief of the *National Review*, "is not necessarily a permanent thing in a dynamic society, and there is no reason for American conservatives to believe either that their hearts deceived them in telling them he [Goldwater] was right, or that the time will never come again when the American people can correct our public policies."

Unlike the rest of the Republicans, the Goldwater forces did not seem particularly discouraged.

"A party that polls over twenty-five million votes," said former Senator William F. Knowland of California, "is neither bankrupt nor on its deathbed."

Goldwater and his followers seemed highly pleased that the Republican vote had exceeded twenty-six million, as if the candidate of one of the two major parties in 1964 could have polled much less, regardless of who the candidate might have been. The fact that Johnson received more than forty-two million votes was left for the moderates and liberals to worry about.

When Senator Goldwater was debating, in the fall of 1963, whether to run for President, he often said that his decision would depend on whether his candidacy would hurt or help the conservative cause. Already the idol of a large and fervent following in the Republican right wing, Goldwater did not want to let the conservatives down by bowing out of the race if by doing so he would take the steam out of the movement. On the other hand, viewing the great popularity of President Kennedy, who was still alive, the senator was hesitant about entering the race if this would mean a severe defeat for the Republican party on election day. This, he believed, would do the conservative cause serious harm and at the same time put the party back in the hands of "me-too" candidates for a long time to come.

When, under heavy pressure, Goldwater announced his candidacy in January, 1964, he evidently had made up his mind that at worst he could win forty-five percent of the popular vote. If he should win the election, so much the better, but if he lost, a showing of this kind, he believed, would strengthen the conservatives permanently. A popular vote of forty-five percent would give them a large base from which to move forward in the future.

When election day came, he received barely thirty-nine percent of the popular vote, which was only a trifle better than Landon's showing in 1936.

What, then, was the effect of this debacle on the right-wing element in the Republican party? Senator Goldwater had campaigned as a conservative. He had offered the people the clearest choice in a generation. He had received the zealous support of right-wing conservatives. Yet he was resoundingly rejected by the majority of the voters. However stoically many of the Goldwater followers may have taken defeat, there is no doubt that millions of Republicans held them to blame for it. In the eyes of a great many voters and in the opinion of many practical Republican politicians the extreme-right-wing cause was discredited. And this was bound to hurt the cause of conservatism generally.

As *The Wall Street Journal* said in an editorial after the election, the Goldwater defeat "also makes it infinitely more difficult as a practical matter for another national politician to fight for conservative views at any time soon; it would be impossible for him to overlook or ignore reminders of what happened in 1964. Regardless of the substance of the matter, the unmistakable appearance is that conservatism has been given a black eye it will be a long time recovering from."

This is probably true, even though the erratic nature of the Goldwater campaign made the election less than a genuine test of the acceptability of traditional conservatism in the United States.

The cause of traditional conservatism in the Republican party suffered unjustly from the association with the Goldwater brand of conservatism, with its emphasis on the negative and its appeal to discontent.

"The Radical Rightist line," as Harry and Bonaro Overstreet say in *The Strange Tactics of Extremism*, "is no more an expression of grass-roots discontent than Bolshevism was an expression of the workers' discontent. It is rather a calculated exploitation of this discontent."

There are signs today of new efforts to put the extreme right in proper perspective. The Overstreet book is a case in point. So is the creation of a committee of eighty prominent Americans under the leadership of Arthur Larson, a former official of the Eisenhower administration and currently director of the World Rule of Law Center at Duke University. Its stated purpose is to expose and correct "the principal errors currently propagated by radical reactionary organizations."

The problem today of the broad, middle-of-the-road, moderate, conservative majority of the Republicans is similar to that of the Democrats nearly a generation ago when their party was seriously embarrassed by the extreme left. The extreme left was not so numerous as the extreme right of today, nor so well endowed with either money or respectability. Furthermore, Soviet postwar expansionism brought discredit on leftists everywhere in the West. The Democrats did not eliminate the extreme left wing, they submerged it. Submerging the extremists is one of the great problems confronting the Republicans now. It will not be easy, partly because, as the Overstreets point out, most middle-of-the-road conservatives have not had as much experience with the tactics of extremists as the Democratic liberals acquired in getting rid of the Communists.

The Johnson landslide seemed to take none of the fervor

out of the extreme right. The Goldwater conservatives have taken over a sector of the Republican party from which they will be dislodged, if at all, only after a long, tough fight. Yet in politics, as in many aspects of American life, success is a great shibboleth. Having failed this test at the polls, the extreme right will not speak in Republican councils with the same authority as before.

A society like the United States will always have extremes of right and left, and the circumstances that gave rise to the right-wing movement will not disappear with the defeat of Senator Goldwater. The racial crisis in the cities will continue for years. Tensions produced by the stalemate with the Soviet Union will increase as Chinese military strength grows. The nostalgia for a simpler past will persist for many years. Many Americans will not get over what sociologist Daniel Bell calls "the inability to take a long historical view of social change." A certain number of people will go on hating restraint, government regulations, and tax obligations. The very fact that the world is moving more rapidly than ever away from old moorings will lend desperation to the tactics of right-wing extremists.

"America," wrote Professor Richard Hofstadter of Columbia University in *Harper's*, "has been largely taken away from them and their kind, though they are determined to try to repossess it and to prevent the final destructive act of subversion. The old American virtues have already been eaten away by cosmopolitans and intellectuals; the old competitive capitalism has been gradually undermined by socialist and communist schemers; the old national security and independence have been destroyed by treasonous plots, having as their most powerful agents not merely outsiders and foreigners as of old but major statesmen who are at the centers of American power. Their predecessors had discovered conspiracies; the modern radical right finds conspiracy to be betrayal from on high."

Many who felt this way before the election may be con-

72

firmed and strengthened in their opinions by the defeat of Senator Goldwater. In time the Republican majority will put things in proportion, but it will not be easy and it may not be soon.

The extreme right is weakened not emotionally perhaps but tactically by the Goldwater defeat. As Goldwater's influence in the party fades, the right wingers will be as hard up as the moderates for leadership. There is no second level of national leaders on the right, no obvious successor to the Goldwater mantle. There have always been differences among right-wing groups, just as among left-wing organizations. It may well come about, therefore, as some of the Goldwater followers fear, that his defeat will lead in time to a fragmentation of the right.

6

THE REPUBLICAN PARTY has been left in such a dire state of collapse by the Goldwater defeat that the effective functioning of the two-party system—that vital safeguard of individual freedom—will be impaired, possibly for years to come.

Whatever Americans of different political persuasion may think of the outcome of the election, few will be pleased with the gross political imbalance that was almost certain to be the consequence of the decision at San Francisco.

The two-party system, with its checks and balances, has been an indispensable contribution to the success of democracy in the United States. While the Constitution is the basis of free government in this country, many other nations with splendid constitutions have fallen, sometimes more than once since 1776. It is not the Constitution alone, but the American political system developed under the Constitution that has fostered the growth of democracy as Americans know it. Essential to that system has been the intercourse and rivalry between the two parties.

Some of the more infamous episodes in American history occurred in times during which the two-party system was out of balance, as it is today.

One of the worst examples was the Reconstruction period. In the electoral college the Republicans were winning Presidential elections by lopsided margins like two hundred and fourteen to eighty and two hundred and eighty-six to forty-two, and undeterred by effective opposition, were imposing such oppression on the South that the party has not been restored there even now, as the election returns of 1964 show. The weakness of the Democratic opposition in the 1920's left the Republicans all the freer to engage in their special follies of that era. And in the mid-1930's the collapse of the Republican party, so vividly brought to mind by the recent debacle, enticed the Democrats into overconfidence, which, on the morrow of the Goldwater defeat, has a moral for Lyndon B. Johnson.

Bloated with votes, President Johnson will ride high, wide, and handsome. Who else can interpret the mandate? As one skeptical observer remarked after the Democrats had carried every state but Maine and Vermont in 1936, "The people have spoken, and in the fullness of time Roosevelt will tell us what they have said." Or as H. L. Mencken remarked of Roosevelt after the returns were in that year, the President "must be entertaining certain stealthy qualms. He now carries all the burdens of omnipotence."

The weakness of the one party and the overwhelming power of the other will surely reduce the quality of debate between the parties. Indeed the unlamented campaign of 1964 was proof enough that it already has. Lopsided victory is not necessarily an unmixed blessing for the victor. Franklin Roosevelt made his worst blunders in the exuberant years following the 1936 landslide. Overestimating the popularity of the New Deal at that stage, he plunged ahead and introduced the court-packing bill. The disastrous effect on public opinion strengthened his opposition in Congress and produced the coalition of Southern Democrats and Northern Republicans that hacked away at his domestic programs and those of Truman later on.

In the 1938 congressional elections Roosevelt sallied grandly forth to purge conservative Democrats like Millard Tydings of Maryland and Walter F. George of Georgia. The results were spectacularly bad. Not only were his Democratic tormentors returned to office but also the Republicans increased their own strength in both houses, and hand-in-hand these two conservative forces offered the strongest challenge Roosevelt had faced since becoming President.

In the 1950's, when Lyndon Johnson was Majority Leader of the Senate and another Democrat, Sam Rayburn, was Speaker of the House, they contributed a good deal of help to the Republican administration. On a number of occasions, mostly involving foreign-policy measures, more Democrats than Republicans supported Eisenhower in Congress, which irked the President no end, welcome though the Democratic votes were.

The kind of problems President Johnson will confront in the next few years are such that he would benefit by sound criticism and fresh ideas from a constructive opposition. Johnson is still new to dealing with world affairs as President. Most of his legislative experience and most of his first eleven months in the White House were concerned mainly with domestic and political problems. But now he is pressed by difficulties abroad.

The departure of Khrushchev and the entry of China into the nuclear club posed delicate questions of American relations with the Communist bloc. The NATO alliance is entering still another phase. Europe is changing steadily and the reunification of Germany comes increasingly to the fore. The task of containing China is already of major concern to the government. Difficult decisions will have to be made about South Vietnam. Johnson does not have a technical or academic background in these matters or long practical experience in dealing with them at first hand. These are problems from which his administration would benefit by responsible and vigorous two-party debate.

At home it is going to take an immense effort to provide the Negroes with a decent standard of living, for this is the goal to which the country is surely committed now. The ceaseless growth of the cities has created a need for decent housing, education, transportation, and medical care. Keeping inflation under control and merely staying abreast of the problem of automation and unemployment will be large orders for the new administration. In the next four to eight years the federal government will have to take steps that will affect the future shape of American civilization.

A strong two-party system would provide the clash of ideas that would help to produce the best thought behind these measures. The two-party system has an additional value at a time like this. The people tend to accept controversial decisions with better grace if they have been hammered out in meaningful debate between the Democrats and Republicans. This was true of the wide range of foreign-policy measures like the Marshall Plan, and more recently it was true of the civil-rights bill.

"The hard fact is," as Arthur Schlesinger, Jr., wrote in 1950, "that while Democrats may gain short-run benefits from the present absence of competition, thoughtful members of that party understand the long-run dangers from absence of competition. An essential function of a party in our system is to secure the concurrence in our political processes of that part of the community which it represents, and if a party becomes so feeble and confused that it turns into an object of public pity or contempt, it can no longer assist in securing that concurrence. As a result our whole political fabric suffers. . . ."

Currently one of the impediments to the checks and balances of the two-party system is that thorough investigation of the Democratic administration is next to impossible because of the seemingly endless minority status of the Republicans in Congress. The majority party controls the committees that conduct investigations. As the Bobby Baker case suggests, the party in power, even when forced into an investigation by public opinion, has a vested interest in limiting the scope of the inquiries before disclosures become too damaging.

Both parties play the game much the same way. If the Democrats had controlled Congress in 1948, it is doubtful whether the investigation of Alger Hiss would have gone as far as it did. And if the Republicans had been in control in 1958, there might not have been an investigation of Sherman Adams.

The Senate's permanent Subcommittee on Investigations is going into the new session of Congress with little of consequence on its agenda other than the winding up of some old inquiries, including the TFX aircraft and other minor matters.

At its best the two-party system is a spur to reform, which is something that may be woefully lacking in the next few years. After the heartwarming returns of November 3, the Democrats are likely to find that things are going altogether too well for anyone to be bothering his head about reform or innovation.

President Johnson's victory ensures that the Democrats will occupy the White House at least through 1968, which means twenty-eight years in office for the Democrats out of the last thirty-six, or something very close to the position of the party of government in this era. The price of this to the Democratic party could be the drying up of many of its own sources of ideas and reform.

An important ingredient of a strong two-party system in the past has been the fact that most of the time the two parties have been rather close to one another on most of the basic issues.

Because the two parties make a nationwide appeal, they have had to be broad enough organizations to embrace the various regions of a continental nation of multifarious races, occupations, creeds, and interests. Historically both parties have represented a consensus of all these interests. The parties have been loose amalgamations of groups rather than neatly labeled bodies of liberals on the left and conservatives on the right. The American system has worked to bring the two parties close together on fundamentals so that their disagreements have usually been over methods rather than goals. Inasmuch as each party has been roughly a coalition of similar interests, it has been difficult for either of the parties to claim sovereignty over the main positions of the day.

The revolution that occurred in the Republican party at San Francisco changed this in 1964. The two parties became separated on the Negro problem, on military policy, on the question of sociopolitical reforms of the last generation, and indeed, to get to the heart of the matter, on the meaning of the Constitution itself. There was a deeper philosophical cleavage between the two parties in the 1964 campaign than in any other since 1896.

On top of that the Republicans nominated a candidate whose appeal was largely sectional. Philosophical cleavage plus sectionalism were bound to have a weakening effect on the two-party system. The nomination of Senator Goldwater lessened the similarity between the parties, as he most eagerly hoped it would. As far as the operations of the two-party system were concerned the effect was the same as it would have been if the Democrats had nominated an extreme-left-wing liberal.

One of the chief elements of the strength of the two-party system lies in the fifty Democratic and fifty Republican parties in the states.

The units of a political party are in the states. In the years of Democratic dominance in Washington, for example, the local and state branches of the Republican party continue to function. Local and state Republican officeholders retain their jobs. Republican leadership and Republican activities help to keep new men and new ideas flowing through the party's veins to give it strength for another attempt to win national power.

As a result of the election of 1964, however, the Republican party has been greatly weakened in a number of states

79

by the loss of legislatures, some of which, as in New York, it had controlled for many years. It has also been weakened in a number of states now torn with strife between Goldwater and anti-Goldwater factions contending for supremacy. The strength that the Republicans ordinarily may look to in the states, therefore, is sapped this year along with its national power.

For a long time, regardless of their relative standing in Washington, the Republicans maintained strong organizations at least in New England and the Midwest. Now it appears that the old one-party Republican states of the North are as much an anachronism as the former one-party Democratic states of the South. Superimposed on their gains of previous years, the Democratic majorities in 1964 produced an entrenched power of formidable dimensions. Even in a free country it is difficult to oust entrenched leadership, whether it is the leadership of James A. Hoffa, James O. Eastland, or James M. Watson. Even independent-minded citizens who voted against Goldwater realized that they may have been helping to make the Democratic party too strong. Yet the "choice" offered by Goldwater had the effect of forcing these voters to put first things first. If the alternatives were giving President Johnson too much power or electing a man whose usage of Presidential power would have been those implied in the Goldwater campaign, then the strengthening of the Republican party had to await a later day. This was not a decision made by Democrats only. It was a decision made by millions of Republicans who voted for President Johnson.

It is not only in the reduced Republican numbers in Congress that the weakening of the two-party system will be felt in the next few years. It is also in the predictable monopoly of the Democrats in radio, television, and the press. The shrunken Republican party will have a hard time being heard except on those newsy occasions when Republicans are fighting each other in Congress, in the Republican National Committee, and in the state capitals.

In the years following the last Presidential inauguration the Kennedy family showed what could be done to black out the opposition. There were months on end when the cover of almost every national magazine featured one Kennedy or another. The glamour and glitter of Jack, Jackie, Bobby, Teddy, Sarge, John-John, Caroline, Macaroni, Ethel, Eunice, Joan, Jean, Pat, and even Charlie (the terrier who chased the ducks into the pond on the south lawn of the White House) so much absorbed public attention that there was little interest left in what the Republicans in Congress were doing.

The Johnson family does not have a hold on press and television in quite the same way. Nevertheless it is not the least of President Johnson's political talents that he is a great propagandist. He will not get the same mileage out of a Pablo Casals concert in the East Room that the Kennedys did perhaps, but he will know in his own way how to exploit the news value of the Presidency.

There will be no member of the minority who will be able to speak for the Republicans with anything like the authority with which Johnson can speak for the Democrats. With the opposition in its weak and divided state the President will know well enough how to keep the Republicans off balance, how to play one faction against the other. It is not hard to imagine how he will be able to stir up the easily aroused right wing by bestowing favors on the moderates. Surely he has not forgotten how, as in the case of the nominations of Stimson and Knox to his Cabinet, Roosevelt used the power of appointment to keep the Republicans at each other's throats. If and when the Republican party comes up with a new idea, the President will not be slow to appropriate it, as with great aplomb he appropriated Goldwater's suggestion that a portion of federal tax revenues be returned to the states. No one will show more sympathy for the troubles of the Republicans: he'll smother them with it.

In the Senate and the House the minority representation will be too small and, for the most part, too lacking in distinction to give the Republican party the decisive voice it needs.

Though the party long ago would have profited from a new production with an entirely different set of words and lyrics, it looks as though the "Ev and Charlie Show" will be back on the boards at the start of the Eighty-ninth Congress. There seems to be no way out of this harlequinade. It is part of the price of adversity. It is part of the price that the Republicans must pay when their weakness makes them no longer a threat to the Democratic party but to the democratic order itself.

7

THERE REMAIN in practically all parts of the country areas of Republican strength, present and potential. It takes a good deal of poking around in the political ruins to find them, and even the best instances must be accompanied by the proviso that an enormous rebuilding job lies ahead before the party can be brought back to normal.

For the election was a setback for the party everywhere, even in the South, where Senator Goldwater scored his only conquest except for Arizona. But in a number of states—in New England, in the Midwest, and in the West, sections that were swept clean by President Johnson—the Republican party still has enduring strength, strength that will yield victories in future elections. The party also still has potential strength in the South. Ironically, however, the five Southern states Goldwater carried are probably the least secure for the Republicans of any of the eleven states in that area.

Since World War II Republicans had achieved notable gains in the South. Although making his best showing there, Goldwater reversed the pattern of these earlier gains in a manner that will hurt the Republicans in the long run. At one time or another, Eisenhower or Nixon had carried Virginia, Florida, Texas, and Tennessee, states that are less distinctively regional than the Deep South. Goldwater, by comparison, lost all these states but did carry the Deep South—Alabama, Mississippi, Louisiana, South Carolina, and Georgia.

In terms of future Republican growth, he carried all of them for the wrong reason. The white voters in these states voted for Goldwater as a protest against the action of the Democratic administration in Washington in broadening the rights of Negroes. This was unfortunate for the Republicans in many respects.

For one thing it dramatized the fact that outside his home state Goldwater could win only in states where a racist appeal overcame every other issue. This has the effect of making the Republican party all the less congenial to Negro voters everywhere.

Goldwater owed his victories in these states to the Black Belt, those rural counties in the Deep South where Negroes constitute a substantial proportion of the population but are effectively prevented from voting. White supremacy is the goal of white voters in the Black Belt. When the Democratic party was the white man's party of the South and protected it against federal intervention, the Black Belt voted Democratic, even in 1928, when Hoover was carrying many other parts of the South against Al Smith. When it appeared that the Democrats would not protect the South against federal intervention in racial affairs, as in 1948, when the party adopted a strong civil-rights plank at Philadelphia, the Black Belt bolted. It voted that year for the Dixiecrat ticket headed by Thurmond. Then in 1964 it cast an angry protest for Goldwater.

Apart from Georgia the South that Goldwater carried was the Dixiecrat South—the same states that had voted for Thurmond in 1948: Alabama, Mississippi, Louisiana, and South Carolina.

Goldwater pulled the Republican party up in the rural areas of the Deep South, but he dragged it down in the cities. In Atlanta, Charlotte, Richmond, Orlando, Houston, and the other metropolitan centers of the South he ran less well than Eisenhower and Nixon. He helped the party in the backward regions but hurt it in progressive, industrialized urban areas. The cities and the suburbs in which Republican strength had begun to show impressively under Eisenhower and Nixon went Democratic in 1964 with the help of the Negro vote, which adds up to less than a happy augury for Republican prospects in the South.

As Professor Donald S. Strong, a political scientist at the University of Alabama, put it, Goldwater "carried a different South" from the South that Eisenhower and Nixon had carried—a South, Strong noted, in which there was "but one issue, segregation." In other words, Republican strength in the South did not increase, its center of gravity simply shifted to the Deep South in line with the segregationist appeal of the party's Southern strategy.

Seen in the light of the 1964 election returns, the South is sharply divided. On one side is the surprisingly Republican Deep South unified by the racial issue. On the other side is the new industrial South, which in its strong Democratic tendencies resembles the border states. One South is striving to remain apart from the rest of the nation on the question of race; the other is tending to become more like the rest of the country on this and other issues.

Voters in the cities who had an interest in economic issues that exceeded their interest in the racial question voted for Johnson. Voters in rural areas who were more interested in white supremacy and less interested in economic issues voted for Goldwater. Although reviving the segregationist Dixiecrat forces under the Republican label, Goldwater thus set back the healthy growth of Republicanism and the two-party system in much of the South.

"Goldwater did the Republican party no favor in the South," says Chancellor Alexander Heard of Vanderbilt University, one of the preeminent students of Southern politics. "He has retarded the development of the Republican party everywhere, including the South."

The population of the rural South has been declining at a faster rate than the population of the rest of rural America.

On the other hand, the urban South is growing at a greater rate than the rest of urban America. What Goldwater succeeded in doing in the South, therefore, was to strengthen the Republican party in areas of population decline and weaken it in areas of population growth.

Many voters in the Southern cities who had voted Republican in the Presidential elections of 1952, 1956, and 1960 would have done so again in 1964 if they had been given the choice of a candidate like Eisenhower or Nixon. But like kindred voters in the Northern cities, they were frightened away by Goldwater.

Since a sweep of the South was essential to Goldwater's strategy for winning the Presidency, the loss of six Southern states—Texas, Virginia, Tennessee, Florida, North Carolina, and Arkansas—was fatal. Of the one hundred and twenty-eight electoral votes of the eleven Southern states, Goldwater received only forty-seven, as compared with Johnson's eighty-one. While Goldwater picked up more electoral votes in the South than Nixon's thirty-three in 1960, he fell below Eisenhower's fifty-seven in 1952 and sixty-seven in 1956.

Apart from the five states carried by Goldwater the Democrats made substantial gains in the South, often reversing promising Republican trends. A most serious Republican setback was the loss of Virginia, Florida, and Tennessee, all of which Nixon had carried in 1960. Illustrative of the extent of this reversal, Virginia gave Nixon nearly fifty-three percent of its vote in 1960 but Johnson more than fifty-five percent in 1964. The turnabout in Tennessee was even greater.

Postwar Republican growth in Texas was brought to a sharp halt by Johnson's landslide in his native state. The Republicans lost their two Texas congressmen, one of whom was Representative Bruce Alger, an extreme conservative from Dallas. With Johnson in the White House for the next four or eight years the Republicans will be up against a crafty and powerful effort to keep Texas firmly under Democratic control.

The Goldwater vote in the Deep South elected six Republicans from Alabama and Mississippi to the House of Representatives, which was the first time that either state had sent a Republican to Congress since the Reconstruction period. Even in this case, however, the gain for the Republican party nationally is dubious. These seven, joined by Thurmond, will constitute a Republican racist clique on Capitol Hill that will cause the Republican party the kind of embarrassment that the Democrats have long suffered from at the hands of their legislators from the Deep South.

The Goldwater folly of ignoring the Negro vote was apparent everywhere outside the Deep South and will add enormously to the Republicans' task of creating a two-party South. In the eleven Southern states there are an estimated two million Negro voters in a voting population of some thirteen million. It was not so very long ago that Negroes were practically the only Republicans in the South. Even as recently as 1960 Nixon received about one third of the Southern Negro vote; Eisenhower did even better. In Atlanta, for example, Nixon received more than half the Negro vote. When Goldwater was nominated, however, the Negroes fled from the Republican party. As was the case in other parts of the country, Johnson received virtually the solid Negro vote in the South. The turnout in some Negro areas of the South was double what it had been in 1960. The Negro vote was crucially important in swinging Virginia, Florida, and Tennessee back to the Democratic party. In Virginia, for example, some Negro precincts that had cast less than sixty percent of their votes for Kennedy gave Johnson more than ninety percent. In certain typical Negro precincts of North Carolina the vote rose from seventy-six percent for the Democrats in 1960 to eighty-seven percent in 1964.

During the Eisenhower administration the Republicans

made an energetic effort to develop state organizations in the South that would appeal to voters regardless of race. On taking over, the Goldwater machine threw out many of the best Eisenhower leaders, notably Robert R. Snodgrass in Georgia, and substituted lily-white organizations in which Republicans often were replaced by renegade Southern Democrats looking for a good thing.

When the Republicans lost practically the entire Negro vote in the South, they put themselves under a staggering handicap for the future. With every year that passes the Negro vote in the South will grow, as more and more Negroes register with the assistance of the federal government and private groups. In many states the Negro vote will be the decisive factor in determining the outcome of elections. By chasing after a Northern white-"backlash" vote that never materialized the Republicans drove from their ranks in states like Virginia a source of strength that had enabled them not only to compete with the Democrats but also to defeat them in Presidential elections.

For all Goldwater's pains, Republican success in Alabama, Mississippi, South Carolina, and Louisiana is likely to be short-lived. After what happened in 1964 the party will surely turn in 1968 to some candidate who will make more of a traditional Republican appeal. Affronted, the Deep South will not find this the kind of choice Goldwater offered and will either return to the Democratic party or march away under a new Dixiecrat banner, or do both.

"In this election," as the Baltimore *Sun* said in an editorial, "the Republican party has managed only to set temporary foot upon the shifting racist sands of the South, and that is a triumph neither for Republicanism nor conservatism. As a base of power, puny at best, it is destined to wither and die."

The ephemeral nature of its gain in the Deep South makes it imperative for the Republicans to begin taking up where they left off in the Eisenhower-Nixon era. The party, if it moves in a sane direction, still has a potential in Presidential elections in states like Florida, Texas, Arkansas, Tennessee, North Carolina, and Florida.

Even without Goldwater progress was maddeningly slow for the Republicans in the South. "For decades," as political scientist James MacGregor Burns writes in *The Deadlock of Democracy*, "political analysts have been predicting a two-party South and Southerners have been perversely failing to vindicate the prophets."

This has been particularly exasperating to the Republicans because conditions in much of the South are favorable to the establishment of a two-party system. In recent years, particularly since the start of World War II, regionalism has been waning in the South. New airports and four-lane highways make Southern states accessible. Southerners watch the same programs and hear the same political speeches on television that Northerners do. With glass-and-steel skyscrapers rising in Atlanta, Dallas, Houston, Richmond, and New Orleans, the South looks more and more like the North.

The South is moving from its predominantly agricultural past into a modern industrial future and in the process a new class of managers and technicians is rising. Business and professional men are moving in from the North and bringing their Republicanism with them. The educational level of the South is rising. People are making more money and building homes in suburbs. All of these factors are helping to create conditions in which the Republican party should flourish. Because much of the South is becoming like the rest of the country, logically it should have two strong parties as have the other sections of the country.

The trouble is, as Professor Burns points out, that the social and economic forces in the South simply have not been converted into the logical political trends. The South has its industry, its cities, its suburbs, its education, its executive class, but somehow these forces have had a delayed impact on politics. Furthermore, for decades the Democrats were so deeply entrenched in Southern courthouses, state houses, governors' mansions, and seats in the Senate and House of Representatives that Republican progress was glacial. And just when it seemed to be accelerating somewhat, the calamity of the Goldwater campaign has slowed it again.

What happened to the Republicans in the South in 1964 at least has its lessons, if the party cares to heed them.

One thing that is clear is that in the future the Republicans must decide *which* South they are appealing to—the backward rural areas that voted for Goldwater or the modern cities that voted for Eisenhower, Nixon, and Johnson. If the latter, then the appeal cannot successfully be based on racial prejudice. Goldwater's loss of eighty-one Southern electoral votes outside the Deep South shows that a Presidential candidate cannot carry the South on the civil-rights issue alone. It was an interesting sidelight on the 1964 election that all eight of the Southern members of the House of Representatives who voted for the civil-rights bill were reelected.

The South is not all rigidly conservative by any means. On any number of issues in Congress over the years its representatives have differed, with many of them voting with the liberals. The racial issue is important in the South; however, it is not the only issue or in many states even the overriding issue. In much of the South it is coming into a new perspective. A great many Southerners recognize that the civil-rights bill was passed as a result of a national consensus, and that no one, not even Goldwater if he had wished to, could repeal it.

The Republicans under a moderate candidate can stand for national policies that will have an appeal in Atlanta, Richmond, Houston, and Charlotte. The Republicans can rebuild in the North in a way that need not alienate the more progressive Southern states. The election returns suggest that the more urbanized Southern states certainly respond to many of the same issues that influence the rest of the country. Republican policies and a Republican candidate who succeed in strengthening the Republican party in the North, as Eisenhower did when he was a candidate, will have a similar bracing effect on the party in the South. The party will have to offer an appeal to economic conservatism that is not based on racism. Furthermore, because of the growing political strength of the Negro, it will have to bid for Negro votes in the South. At best it may be a long time before such a bid produces any substantial number of votes.

Reapportionment of the Southern legislatures is giving the moderates relatively greater power. This makes it all the more important that the Republican party should make the same appeal to the South that it makes to the North. It is interesting to note the changing tone of the intercourse between the governors of the Southern states. At the Southern governors' conference in San Antonio a month before the 1964 election, the word "segregation" was not mentioned at any session. Governor Wallace, instead of advocating defiance of the federal government as had been his custom, limited himself to introducing a mild resolution proposing a constitutional amendment that would relieve the Supreme Court of any jurisdiction over schools. The governors spent a good deal more time discussing the application of nuclear power to Southern industries.

The clear meaning of the election returns is that there is no significant place in the South for what Strom Thurmond frankly called "the Goldwater Republican party" during the campaign.

It is not only in the South but also in all sections of the country that assessment of Republican strength has to be qualified with words like "potential" and "latent." The party is in eclipse. There are no very bright spots, yet there are areas of enduring strength that may grow slowly, some more so than others. The party suffered the way it did in 1964 because millions of voters, including Republicans, voted against Goldwater and not against the Republican party. When the Republicans nominate a more characteristic type of candidate, they will win back many voters who voted for President Johnson.

Maine, New Hampshire, and Vermont are states that the Republicans will win again. A new generation and changed circumstances have simply ended the Republican monopoly on them. In Maine, for example, the legislature went Democratic in 1964 for the first time in half a century. New Hampshire and Vermont have Democratic governors. But in each of the three states the Republicans are either in the majority or close to it.

Johnson's victory in the Midwest was the greatest since the 1936 Roosevelt landslide, but it was abnormal. The Republicans still have a strong foundation in such states as Ohio, Indiana, Nebraska, Kansas, Minnesota, Wisconsin, Illinois, and North and South Dakota. Governor Romney in Michigan was reelected, though that was more of a personal victory than a Republican one. The Republicans are weak in Michigan, but they are stronger in neighboring states than appeared in the Johnson landslide.

It was probably only because of Goldwater that Robert Taft, Jr., lost the Senate race in Ohio and Charles H. Percy failed to win the governorship in Illinois. Each made a strong showing under the circumstances. The Republicans elected governors in Kansas, Wisconsin, and South Dakota.

The Republicans control the legislature in Kansas and Ohio and at least one of the houses of the legislatures in several other Midwestern states.

For the usual reason the party lost the Rocky Mountain states in 1964, but it has enough strength in this region to justify hopes for revival. Idaho, Colorado, Arizona, and Montana have Republican governors. On the West Coast the Republicans elected a promising young governor of Washington and a United States senator in California.

In states like Delaware, New Jersey, and Pennsylvania it

is not farfetched to imagine a Republican comeback with some luck, hard work, and good candidates. Despite the Johnson landslide the Republicans in Pennsylvania re-elected Hugh Scott as senator and held one house of the legislature. Governor Scranton will be in office until 1966 to push the work of rebuilding.

None of these areas of potential Republican strength does anything to alter the catastrophic nature of the party's loss in the 1964 election. Indeed they look almost pathetic against the overall statistics of the Democratic victory. Nonetheless, they are part of the post-election political picture. The Republican party will have to start out again on a long climb, and these are likely places to begin.

8

ALTHOUGH THE STRUGGLE for control of the Republican party has now reached a new peak of intensity in the aftermath of one of the party's worst defeats, it is in fact the continuation of decades of political warfare between the conservatives and the liberals to possess the soul, to define the purposes, and to choose the leaders of the party.

Nearly thirty years ago the intraparty conflict reminded Alfred Landon of "two undertakers quarreling over a corpse." In 1949 Thomas E. Dewey, having lost the second of two campaigns for the Presidency, said at a dinner on Lincoln's birthday, "The Republican party is split wide open. It has been split wide open for many years, but we have tried to gloss it over."

The split remains, deeper than ever, but at least there is no longer any effort to gloss it over. From the day after the Johnson landslide the two sides have been hurling themselves at one another without respite. Neither side has the preponderance of strength to drive off the other, and the two are largely irreconcilable. Barring some event not now manifest, therefore, the struggle will go on for years.

Its immediate phase centers on the roles of Barry Goldwater and his close friend and former senatorial assistant, Dean Burch, a young, energetic, incisive, attractive Tucson attorney whom Goldwater chose as Republican national chairman.

"Senator Goldwater," said Robert Corber, Republican

state chairman of Virginia, after the election, "has been completely repudiated at the polls. He should not be the leader of the party under any circumstances." But, of course, Goldwater will be the titular leader of the Republican party for the next few years, and he may try to be a fairly aggressive one at that. "I'll have a lot of time to devote to this party, to its leadership, and to the strengthening of the party, and that I have every intention of doing," he said the day after the election.

A stormy time awaits him in this role. His candidacy was too disastrous for the party, his opinions too controversial for him to attempt any leadership worthy of the name without arousing harsh conflict. The history of the difficulties and frustrations that have beset other nominal leaders of the Republican party offers him little hope of anything different.

As a defeated candidate Hoover succeeded in winning control over the Republican National Committee and using it to propagate his own views. But he was balked when he tried to get Republican congressional leaders to fall in line with his opinions, and he failed in his efforts to use his role as a stepping-stone to renomination. When Landon in turn became titular leader he got into angry quarrels with Hoover, and for a time the two men were not even on speaking terms. Landon blocked Hoover's attempts to extend his influence over the party, yet he too was ineffectual in guiding Republican policy in Congress. Fiery controversy was Willkie's hallmark as titular leader. For trying to steer the party away from isolationism he was publicly repudiated by Republicans in Congress. Between 1944 and 1948 Dewey retained a fair amount of influence because of his powerful organization based in New York but still found the limits of maneuver narrow for the titular leader. "I have held that title in my party now for nearly six years," he observed in 1950, "and I still have some doubts about what it means except that I am the last duly nominated spokesman for my party."

After Nixon was defeated in 1960 he gave a good deal of thought to serving as a full-time Republican national chairman with a sizable opposition-party apparatus established along British lines. Before pursuing the idea he decided to seek the approval of General Eisenhower, who had not yet left office. When Eisenhower displayed no particular interest, Nixon let it drop. As will surely happen to Goldwater, Nixon as titular leader was caught in a crossfire between the two wings of his party, each of which felt, for opposite reasons, that he had waged a poor campaign. After he was defeated for governor of California in 1962, whatever prestige he had as nominal leader was largely dissipated.

Goldwater will fare no better than his predecessors. While he will retain a friendly following among hard-core conservatives, the rest of the party will take the view that he and his philosophy have been repudiated by the voters. After January 3, 1965, he no longer will be a member of the Senate. He will not hold any elective office to provide a base such as Dewey had when he was titular leader and governor of New York. It is difficult to imagine any major national issue on which Goldwater's views will make a significant impact, and he will have no more success than his predecessors in influencing Republican policy in Congress.

Yet he emerged from defeat determined to go on fighting for his brand of Republicanism. The moment a cry went up in other quarters of the party for Burch's resignation, Goldwater opposed it, contending that the chairman had done "a very, very commendable job." "My recommendation would be to keep him," the senator said, "because for the first time in memory we finished the campaign in the black."

Ordinarily Republicans would be pleased to end a campaign with a surplus, but after the 1964 election Goldwater's foes were suspicious that money that might otherwise have been spent to help Republican Senate and House candidates was hoarded for an ulterior purpose. This purpose, it was suspected, was to have the surplus on hand as a lever to enable Burch and the Goldwater group to retain control of the Republican National Committee.

In fact, the suspicion that Goldwater was plotting to keep control of the party even in defeat has been rife among the moderate Republicans ever since San Francisco. It increased with the appointment of Burch, a politician of limited experience who had never even been a county chairman and who was a complete stranger to hundreds of eminent Republicans around the country. When, after Burch was installed as national chairman, the same kind of zealotry that had carried Goldwater to the nomination flooded into the National Committee headquarters, it looked more than ever as if the extreme right was digging in for a long stand in Washington.

John Grenier, a young politician from Alabama, was appointed executive director. When he arrived at national headquarters, it was reported, he ordered pictures of Lincoln and Eisenhower taken down. Later he relented. Established members of the committee staff were dismissed or demoted and replaced by persons whose loyalty to Goldwater was unquestioned.

Of all Burch's actions, the one that aroused the deepest suspicion among the other wing of the party was his appointment in mid-September, 1964, of a new executive committee of the National Committee, long before the selection was necessary and without any wide consultation, evidently, among the full membership of the National Committee.

The sudden dropping of such veteran executive-committee members as George L. Hinman of New York, George F. Etzell of Minnesota, Harley B. Markham of Idaho, Robert L. Pierce of Wisconsin, Mrs. Albert S. Koeze of Michigan,

Charles E. Whittenmeyer of Iowa, and Robert R. Snodgrass of Georgia shocked even the professionals in the moderate wing. In their eyes this was a gesture almost as tough, nonconciliatory, and uncompromising as the Goldwater acceptance speech and the nomination of William Miller. When, for example, they saw New York, Wisconsin, and Michigan knocked off the executive committee and Mississippi, Louisiana, and Arizona added, they thought they had a clear indication which way the wind was blowing.

Among those appointed were a recognized segregationist and certain national committeewomen of little distinction and less acquaintance among the older members of the National Committee. Members of the previous executive committee who were not considered conservative enough by Goldwater standards were ousted. "They made you write your name in blood," one committee official said. The professionals in the other camp viewed the new executive committee as a selection by Burch of lesser-known figures on whose votes he would be able to count in a showdown. In the normal course of things carrying the vote of the executive committee gives the chairman a good start toward getting his way with the larger National Committee.

However, the experience of some recent Republican national chairmen after an election defeat offers little comfort to Burch.

Following Willkie's defeat Joseph Martin stayed on for a while, but partly because no one else would touch the job under the circumstances. As large contributors shut their wallets, the National Committee went broke. It even suffered the indignity of being evicted from its headquarters by the C.I.O., which owned the building. Martin wrangled with members of the finance committee and wound up paying thousands of dollars of routine committee expenses out of his own pocket. "For my pains I was attacked from all sides," he said afterward.

Even more ominous for Dean Burch's future is the case of Hugh Scott, who—while a representative from Pennsylvania—served as the Republican national chairman at the time the party was rocked by Truman's defeat of Dewey in 1948. The same demands for Burch's scalp broke about Scott's immediately after the election. Enraged Republicans wanted to throw him out even though it was not Scott but Herbert Brownell, Dewey's campaign manager, who had run the campaign. Still, Scott had been Dewey's choice for national chairman, as Burch was Goldwater's.

When the members of the National Committee arrived in Omaha for a meeting in January, 1949, a bitter fight broke out to remove Scott. Somewhat the way anti-Goldwater Republicans are talking about Burch nowadays, Scott's foes called him a "symbol of Dewey misrule." They also charged him with packing the executive committee, which is very likely something about which Burch will be hearing more.

Scott stubbornly refused to resign. At first the National Committee appointed a seven-man "harmony" committee to try to resolve the dispute without further public brawling. After a few hours, however, this effort collapsed because Scott insisted that this group had no jurisdiction over the question of his removal. Then Scott's opponents tried for a compromise. They said that they favored Roy Dunn of Minnesota for the chairmanship but that they would withdraw his name if Scott would resign and allow a third person to be named chairman. Scott would not budge. Just as Burch now enjoys the backing of Goldwater, Scott had the support of Dewey as well as of the Pennsylvania boss, Joe Grundy.

Dunn was duly put forward by backers of Taft, Vandenberg, Stassen, and Lodge, who claimed to have fifty-seven signatures on a petition to declare the office of chairman vacant. The debate went on for hours, as one committee member after another rose to denounce Scott and Dewey. In words that do not sound altogether unfamiliar in today's donnybrook, Walter Hallanan of West Virginia opened the case against Scott, charging, "An election was lost because of stupidity, arrogance, and cockiness." The same might be said of the arraignment of Scott by Harrison Spangler of Iowa, a former national chairman. "We have lost the confidence of the people," Spangler cried. "We are the subject of ridicule on every street corner. We are the laughingstock because we didn't fight. If we endorse that campaign, the party will just evaporate from any position of importance in this country."

Jacob France, the Republican national committeeman from Maryland, finally introduced a motion to declare the chairmanship vacant "in the best interests of the party." By a parliamentary maneuver "to lay it on the table," the resolution was defeated by a vote of fifty-four to fifty. Although Scott had survived "the battle of Omaha," the margin was so slight that his tenure was doomed.

In July that year some twenty-five members of the National Committee, many of them Taft supporters, met privately at the Duquesne Hotel in Pittsburgh and decided to try to force the issue against Scott again. A few days later a small delegation including Leonard Hall and George Bloom of Pennsylvania called on Scott and told him that his position in the committee was hopeless. They asked him to step down rather than get his head bloodied in another fight. This time he consented. In August the Taft forces, led by the late Carroll Reece of Tennessee, once a national committeeman, and Representative Clarence J. Brown of Ohio brought about the election of Guy George Gabrielson of New Jersey as national chairman. After he took over, the money started pouring into the Republican treasury again from contributors who were confident—mistakenly it turned out—that Taft would be nominated in 1952.

Burch too will have to get out sooner or later. After an election as ruinous as that of 1964 the losers cannot hope to retain control of party machinery beyond a point. This is an opinion that is shared without any qualifications at all by at least five recent Republican national chairmen. The purpose of getting rid of Burch when the time comes will be mainly to symbolize the end of Goldwater rule, for control of the National Committee and the chairmanship is not the locus of ultimate power in the party.

The National Committee cannot lay out the course of the party or determine the selection of its Presidential nominee. Between conventions it is essentially, though not exclusively, a housekeeping organization. It has no patronage to speak of. It cannot lay down policy for Republicans in Congress. It cannot dictate to party organizations in the states. It cannot tell Republican governors what to do. If members of the party do not like what the committee does, they may ignore it.

Although the departure of Burch would not be so significant an event as the present clamor for it suggests, nevertheless a new chairman untainted by the 1964 defeat could give the party a voice it has not had since Goldwater lost. A bold and talented chairman can use the National Committee as a forum from which to influence events. When Eisenhower suffered a heart attack in 1955 and the public began to wonder whether the Republicans would have to nominate someone else the next year, Leonard Hall, then the national chairman, took it upon himself to declare, almost before the President was out of the oxygen tent, that Eisenhower would run for a second term. His statement had the effect of conditioning public opinion to accept the idea of a man's running for the Presidency after he had had a heart attack. In the summer of 1956, when there was a good deal of talk about dropping Nixon from the ticket, Hall did much to squelch it by saying that Nixon would be the Vice-Presidential nominee again.

A man who stood out as a strong and effective chairman was the late Paul M. Butler, who was chairman of the Democratic National Committee in the 1950's. It was he who set up the Democratic Advisory Council to make recommendations on policy and programs. The council was formed against the wishes of Speaker Rayburn and Lyndon Johnson, who was Majority Leader of the Senate at the time, and thus it failed to influence Democratic policy in Congress, but it was highly effective in propagandizing issues on which Democratic candidates run for President.

Butler did something else that lies within the reach of a determined national chairman. Although a chairman cannot determine the outcome of a national convention, he can use his power of appointing committees and officials in a way that makes the road easier for a particular candidate. Butler used this power in the interests of John F. Kennedy in 1960, just as William Miller was to do on behalf of Goldwater in 1964, a service that certainly did not militate against his being picked by Goldwater for the Vice-Presidential nomination.

The pressure to elect a new national chairman will come from too many sources to be resisted.

It will come from the group within the National Committee, of whom George Hinman of New York is typical, who are not reconciled to Goldwater's control. (John B. Martin, Republican national committeeman from Michigan, said, "We should start by asking Senator Goldwater to urge Dean Burch, who was chosen as chairman at the senator's request, to resign.")

It will come from liberal Republicans in Congress like Senators Kuchel of California and Case of New Jersey, Representative Lindsay and Senator Javits of New York, and Representatives Mathias of Maryland and Conte of Massachusetts. (Senator Hugh Scott said, "The present party leadership must be replaced—all of it.")

It will come from the large group of middle-of-the-road Republicans who had clustered around General Eisenhower, which would include men like Milton Eisenhower, former Secretary of Interior Fred Seaton of Nebraska, former Assistant Secretary of the Treasury Fred C. Scribner, Jr., of Maine, and former Republican national chairman Meade Alcorn of Connecticut. (Senator Thruston B. Morton of Kentucky, who had been a Republican national chairman during the Eisenhower administration, said, "Dean Burch will have to go. I don't think there'll be too much trouble about that.")

It will come too from Midwestern conservatives who followed Goldwater with enthusiasm until they found that he had led them up a blind alley. (Harry G. Taylor, president of the Illinois Republican Chairman's Association, said, "I think we all feel Burch should go, but it should be done in an orderly fashion. He represents an aura of defeat. When the time comes he should resign for a more moderate, middle-ground spokesman. Most county chairmen feel that way.")

Although Goldwater still has some staunch followers on the committee, his grip on party machinery outside the South has been exaggerated, particularly so in light of the disastrous nature of his defeat. The best evidence points to the fact that many members of the committee who were for Goldwater at San Francisco want to get rid of him and Burch now. National committeemen and state chairmen do not like to string along with a loser. Burch's opponents may not wish to move against him until they can come to some kind of agreement among themselves, but in due time new forces will replace the Goldwater group in control of the National Committee. That will be only the end of a skirmish; the struggle for control of the party will go on.

9

THE Republican party lies in wreckage today because its moderates and liberals failed after the defeat of 1960 to retain their long control over the party's Presidential sector. The moderates succeeded in nominating every Presidential candidate between 1940 and 1960, but they have not had comparable control of the Congressional sector of their party. The future of the Republican party depends to a large extent on whether the moderates can do better in the Presidential sector after the election of 1964.

Despite the termination of eight years of Republican Presidential rule brought about by Kennedy's victory in 1960, the Republican moderates and liberals retained great sources of strength with which to sustain themselves.

Nixon had lost by only a freakishly small plurality. He was only forty-seven years old and still had a large following. President Eisenhower had towering influence in the party if he chose to exercise it. Henry Cabot Lodge, who had been Nixon's running mate, commanded the esteem of a great many Republicans.

The Republican moderates and liberals were rich in governors of states that would send large delegations to the Republican National Convention of 1964. Rockefeller was governor of New York. Scranton was governor of Pennsylvania. Rhodes was governor of Ohio. Romney was governor of Michigan. Among the smaller states there were moderate Republican governors in Colorado, Idaho, Kansas, Maine,

Oregon, and Rhode Island. As a team these governors would have been a hard combination for any right-wing conservative to buck at a convention under ordinary circumstances.

After Nixon's defeat, it is true, talk was heard here and there about running Goldwater next time. But of course those who could sense American public opinion or in fact anyone who troubled to read a Gallup or Harris poll had as much reason to predict then as in the summer of 1964 that electing Goldwater to the White House was unimaginable. Therefore the myth that the convention would never deliberately nominate a loser caused the moderates to underrate Goldwater from the start. His poor showing in the 1964 primaries misled them further. The leaders of the moderates, all except Rockefeller, failed to work as hard or fight as hard as the Goldwater forces. Many of them were willing to put up money but not time and effort. The spirit of the rank and file behind them was pallid compared with the hot-eyed fervor of the Goldwater followers. Instead of working together early enough to get control of the convention, the moderates went their own individual way or hung back or tried to undermine one another until it was too late for any of them. When they finally arrived in San Francisco in July they were in near panic, and Goldwater was nominated on the first ballot.

Now that the party has gone down to defeat and must begin a new search for leadership, the question is whether the moderates have learned their lesson, and if so, what they are going to do about it.

At the outset the trouble is that their well-known leaders are at best shopworn, if not politically finished.

Whatever his motives, General Eisenhower caused such bitter disappointment among the moderates in the months before San Francisco that he has no chance of being a powerful leader among them again. The former President had his own reasons for doing what he did and he was entitled to them, but the above-the-battle posture he adopted left millions of Republicans disgusted and disillusioned. Now approaching seventy-five, he will increasingly withdraw from politics. Younger Republicans coming up will not likely look to him for active leadership.

Rockefeller, who at least emerged from the last convention with the honor that goes with fighting a hard fight, looks to be very close to the end of the political road. The marital question that dogged him through his fight for the 1964 Presidential nomination has been aggravated by the court ruling denying Mrs. Rockefeller custody of her four children. Rockefeller poured everything into his quest for the nomination: his money, his personality, his time, his energy, his fine staff, his family's great record of service, his own record as governor of New York—and still it was not enough. What more could he offer?

On the homestretch of his term as governor of New York, which will expire in 1966, he faces dilemmas that will not make his political fortunes any brighter. The scandals in the State Liquor Authority are still embarrassing, and the state is in financial difficulties. But even if these were not problems enough, the Johnson landslide swept the Democrats into control of the New York state legislature for the first time in more than a quarter of a century. With control of the legislature and with an ambitious new United States senator in the person of Robert F. Kennedy to lend a hand, the Democrats will be out to recapture the governorship in 1966. It is now questionable whether Rockefeller can be reelected, and if his private polls paint a dark picture, he may not even run.

Nixon would no doubt like another shot at the Presidency. He has certain qualifications for the office. He might, though without winning, have run the best race of any Republican against Johnson in 1964. He still seems to be strong in the Midwest. Since the Goldwater smashup a number of party officials around the country have suggested that Nixon would be the man best suited to pick up the pieces for his party in one capacity or another, perhaps as national chairman. His political career now spans two decades. Unless it is Goldwater, no other politician alive has been through such violent controversies. Nixon has made many enemies, and something about the man seems to impel him to make more.

Republicans, he once said, have an "almost cannibalistic urge to destroy and consume one another." Accordingly, two days after the election, he stoked the fire, filled the kettle, and proceeded to try to destroy Nelson Rockefeller. "He has had his pound of flesh," Nixon said, alleging that the governor's lackluster campaign for Goldwater had cost the Republican ticket many votes. If there were some way in which Nixon could convincingly disavow any further ambitions to be President, he undoubtedly would be the best man available to take the lead in putting the party back together. But he has been such an obvious schemer for power that no disclaimer of this kind would stick with his rivals. Encrusted with controversy, surrounded by enemies, burdened with two major defeats, and declining in popularity, Nixon's chances of ever winning the Presidency must be considered poor.

The outlook for Romney and Scranton is harder to judge, but obviously more hopeful than for the others.

Romney has political assets of a high order. He was a successful businessman who rose to the presidency of the American Motors Corporation. While some thought his Mormon background would hurt him in politics, he became in 1962 the first Republican in fourteen years to be elected governor of Michigan. He put through a new constitution and made an excellent record in his first term. At the San Francisco convention he offered from the floor an amendment to the platform repudiating extremist groups, but not by name. The amendment, of course, was shouted down in characteristic fashion by that gathering. On election day, although Goldwater lost Michigan by more than one million votes, Romney won. He has become a popular Republican figure in a state with a large Negro and labor vote. Even though Johnson received 67.7 percent of the popular vote for President in Michigan, 56.3 percent of the state's voters voted for Romney.

In his winning campaign, however, Romney incurred the wrath of the Goldwater following everywhere by refusing to endorse Goldwater or even to mention him in his campaign. Indeed he did not overly emphasize the word "Republican." If the time comes when Romney seeks to extend his power beyond Michigan, he will run into opposition from the right wing of the party. For that matter, many Republican professionals of all breeds are cold on Romney. His loquacious evangelism and his talk about armies of citizens taking over politics make them want to look elsewhere in a hurry. It is therefore debatable whether Romney's obvious appeal in Michigan can be translated into the universal appeal needed to win a Presidential election.

Romney will be sixty-one at the time of the next Republican National Convention. His man-of-distinction appearance would have been an asset against a younger opponent like President Kennedy. It was probably because the contrast in age might have made Romney seem wiser and more experienced that President Kennedy feared him more than any other prospective opponent for 1964. Romney's maturity would be less of an asset against a man of his own age like Johnson. In order to remain in the Presidential picture for 1968 Romney will have to run again in Michigan in 1966, when his term expires. He will unquestionably be the primary target of the Democrats that year. But if they fail to knock him off, he will grow with his victory and will be a leading contender for the next Republican Presidential nomination.

Scranton's problem is more difficult. His term also expires in 1966, but Pennsylvania law prohibits a second term. If he is interested in the 1968 nomination, he will therefore have to find some new theater in which to display his political talents and hold the voters' interests after he retires as governor. Scranton is an able public servant who has made an excellent record in Harrisburg. He is good-looking, he has infectious charm, he is an excellent speaker, he has more high style than any politician since John Kennedy, yet he has probably also raised more doubts about himself than any other politician since Adlai Stevenson.

His handling of himself in 1964 fell abysmally below his own abilities. Creating an image of a man tormented by self-doubt, he would not seek the nomination when there was still a chance he might have won it, and then he went after it when Goldwater had it locked up. He let himself out on a perilous limb at the governors' conference in Cleveland, going on a national television program to say absolutely nothing when the whole country was watching to see him announce his candidacy. At San Francisco he begged the question whether he knew what was going on under his own nose when he confessed that it was not he but a member of his staff who had dispatched a letter over his signature to Goldwater containing a monumental denunciation of all that Goldwater stood for. At the convention this made Scranton anathema to the extreme conservatives. It was unthinkable that he ever again could have got a kind word or a vote out of any of them. Yet when Scranton lost the nomination he went to the podium, spoke well of Goldwater, and moved that Goldwater's nomination be made unanimous.

In the weeks before the election, much to the disgust of some liberals, he campaigned for Goldwater in many states. Unlike Romney and Keating, he remained "regular." In keeping his party credentials in order, he probably recouped some of the losses he had suffered among the conservatives.

Largely as a result of his own doing, the American people

never got a true picture of Scranton in 1964. He is much smarter, more robust, more tenacious, more humorous, more personable than he seemed in his first appearance on the national stage. Whether he knows what he wants now any more than he did then, of course, is another matter. If he does, and if he will act accordingly, rectifying the image he created, he has a good chance of becoming one of the party's foremost leaders in the future.

Besides Romney several moderate Republicans won gubernatorial elections when Goldwater lost: Avery in Kansas, Chafee in Rhode Island, Evans in Washington, and Knowles in Wisconsin. Smylie of Idaho, Love of Colorado, Reed of Maine, and Hatfield of Oregon were not up for reelection in 1964. These men operate from such narrow bases of power, however, that their opportunities for national leadership are limited. A winner who arouses greater interest is Representative John Lindsay of New York.

Lindsay is a tall, lean, handsome, forty-three-year-old lawyer who won his fourth term in the House from Manhattan's "Silk Stocking" district despite a Johnson avalanche. A leader among the Republican liberals in the House, he is despised by many conservatives, but he has long been marked as a comer in New York, where he has the solid backing of what is now known as the "Eastern Establishment." Lindsay's immediate problem is how to break out of the obscurity of the House. It would take years for him to become a national leader from his present post.

Two avenues are open to him. If Rockefeller decides not to run for governor of New York in 1966 and Senator Javits does not run, Lindsay would be the strongest gubernatorial candidate the Republicans could present. The other possible avenue of advancement would be for Lindsay to try for Javits' Senate seat if for any reason the senator were not to run again in 1968. With the Democrats on the way up again in New York, Lindsay's obstacles are formidable. If he could scramble over them to Albany, however, the

Republicans would have a new Presidential contender on their hands. Lindsay's record and appearance, plus his spectacular victory in 1964, have already given him national recognition. Party leaders recognize that Lindsay has some of the same attractive qualities that aided President Kennedy and that Lindsay is the least tarnished of Republican Presidential possibilities.

The kind of leadership implied when such names as Romney, Scranton, Nixon, and Rockefeller are mentioned really is eventual leadership in the party's Presidential sector. But the next nomination is far off. It is a matter of boundless speculation and subject to every conceivable change. Goldwater was probably right when he said at a press conference at Jamaica's Montego Bay ten days after the election, "Anybody who tries to guess now what the party will do in 1968 has to be an idiot." That time will come soon enough, but in the meantime the current leadership of the party will be exercised not by distinguished individuals scattered throughout the states or by governors, though they will be a factor, but by the congressional sector of the Republican party in Washington.

For the time being the problem of the moderates will be not so much how to deal with one another as how to influence Republican policy in Congress and how to cope with President Johnson's maneuvers to preempt on behalf of the Democrats the positions of all liberals, moderates, and conservatives. In an important way, strangely enough, the Johnson landslide strengthened the hand of the Republican moderates in the congressional sector of their party. Though it was rather overlooked in the first reaction to the larger drama, the election may have had a profound effect on the balance of power in the congressional sector of the Republican party, a change that could increase the influence of the moderates. For although the Republican party suffered a net loss of thirty-eight seats in the House, the Republican moderates and liberals came through the election with only a minor decline in numbers. But the staunch conservative Republicans closely identified with Goldwater lost heavily.

Despite the landslide, the Republicans elected moderates like Mailliard and Baldwin of California; Tupper of Maine; Morse of Massachusetts; MacGregor of Minnesota; Grover, Wydler, Halpern, Fino, and Reid of New York; and Mc-Dade, Corbett, Schweiker, Schneebeli, Saylor, and Fulton in Pennsylvania. Goldwater lost in all their districts.

The extreme conservative ranks in the House were reduced by the defeat of pro-Goldwater members like Martin of California; Brotzman of Colorado; McLoskey of Illinois; Wilson of Indiana; Bromwell and Jensen of Iowa; Snyder of Kentucky; Knox of Michigan; Beermann of Nebraska; Wyman of New Hampshire; Wharton of New York; Schenck of Ohio; Short of North Dakota; Foreman of Texas; Goodling of Pennsylvania; Westland, Horan, and Stinson of Washington; Van Pelt of Wisconsin; Harrison of Wyoming; and others.

Ironically, many of these victims of the landslide were among the fifty-four Republican representatives who on June 17 signed a manifesto saying: "We are convinced that the nomination of Senator Barry Goldwater will result in substantial increases in Republican membership in both houses of Congress." With the exception of Arizona, President Johnson carried every one of the states from which fifty-three of the signers came. In addition to the net of thirty-eight seats the Democrats gained in the House, they also picked up two in the Senate.

Liberal Republicans had feared that even though Goldwater might be swamped on election day the very size of the landslide might work to extend his sway over the Republican-party machinery.

The theory was that he would run poorest in the Eastern states where Republican liberals were up for reelection and strongest in the Midwest and West where Democratic lib-

erals were thought to be in jeopardy. The result, if the returns had gone that way, would have meant that Republican liberals would have been thrown out of Congress by
Johnson's Eastern landslide and that Western Republican
conservatives would have been pulled in by Goldwater's
anticipated better showing west of the Alleghenies. Thus it
was feared that conservative Republican Senate candidates
would replace such Democratic liberals as Burdick of North
Dakota, Cannon of Nevada, Hartke of Indiana, McGee of
Wyoming, and Moss of Utah. The same result was feared in
gubernatorial races involving Romney, Chafee, and other
moderate Republican candidates.

"If Mr. Goldwater should be overwhelmed by a Democratic landslide," wrote Alan L. Otten in *The Wall Street
Journal* last September, discussing the possibility of this
outcome, "he could drag down with him a large number of
liberal or moderate Republicans running for governor, senator, representative, or other office in the big industrial
states, while conservative candidates in the South, West,
and other Goldwater country might survive. Thus the
elected face of the Grand Old Party would take on a most
visible conservative cast; far more so than if the Goldwater
loss were narrower and more of the liberals-moderates,
deemed likely to run ahead of Barry in the big industrial
states, were to hold onto power."

But that is not the way it came out. The liberal governors survived. House moderates fared better, relatively,
than the conservatives. And in the Senate Burdick, Cannon,
Hartke, McGee, and Moss defeated their conservative chal-
lengers. Conservative Republican Senate candidates also
lost in Texas, Oklahoma, and New Mexico. Goldwater did
not even get the booby prize of greater conservative majorities in Washington to help him hold on to the party.

The Johnson landslide swept out so many conservatives
that the moderate Republicans won relatively greater
power in the congressional sector of their party, reduced

113

though this sector is. This does not mean that the moderates will have control of the Republican party on Capitol Hill. But they will have a stronger voice. They will have greater leverage for moving the party back toward the middle of the road. Representative Halleck, the Republican leader of the House, and Senator Dirksen, the Republican leader of the Senate, are not doctrinaire. As practical political leaders, they swing with the tides of opinion. They can understand as well as the next fellow the meaning of the Goldwater debacle. They will listen a little more attentively to Senators Kuchel, Case, and Javits, Representatives Lindsay, Cooper, and Ford, and a few others.

The moderates, like all Republicans, have a staggering task ahead of them, but at least San Francisco is behind.

10

WHAT IS WRONG with the Republican party? Why is it that a party that was in power for fifty-six of the seventy-two years prior to 1932 has been in power only eight years out of the past thirty-two and has now lost again?

The answer, obviously, is that a great many things are wrong. The various mistakes and failures have been defined in different ways by different authorities.

"We need now," said former President Eisenhower after the Goldwater defeat, "to consult among ourselves as to methods for correcting the false image of Republicanism which far too long has confused so many of our citizens and led them to think of it as a political doctrine designed primarily for the rich and privileged."

The image of Republicans as the party of "the rich and privileged" is one thing that is wrong. But there are others.

"Clearly," the historian of the Republican party George H. Mayer wrote in surveying the party's troubles in modern times, "the GOP did not make an energetic effort to find new sources of support when the coalition based on Midwestern farmers, big business, and the old middle class lost its numerical importance. Theodore Roosevelt had sensed the need of catering to the rapidly growing working class in the pre-World War I era and had advocated some of the social services for which the Democrats later received credit.

"By mid-twentieth-century standards his approach was tentative and superficial, but it temporarily prevented the drift of underprivileged groups to the Democrats. Although Roosevelt had created new bases for the GOP to build on, it ignored the opportunity in the 1920's and suffered a slow erosion of its support, particularly among the foreign-born in the urban East. This trend was first apparent in 1928, but the Republicans ignored the warning and lost this group as well as the native workers and Negroes in 1932. Thereafter the continued growth of the urban populations, coupled with the decrease of the farm vote, doomed the Republicans to minority status."

"It's a good thing," then Republican national chairman Hugh Scott snapped to a reporter when it was apparent that Truman had defeated Dewey in 1948. "Those mastadons wouldn't listen to me. They had to learn their lesson. Now maybe they'll go out and pass some good social legislation."

He was referring, of course, to the Republican members of the Eightieth Congress who had just wound up two years of speeches savagely attacking the reforms of the New Deal and the Fair Deal.

"The Democrats," Walter Lippmann wrote in assessing the Republican disaster of 1964, "have pre-empted almost all the attractive proposals because they have included so much of the intellectual community which is capable of devising attractive proposals. . . . The Republicans will have to find a way to end their alienation from the best brains of the nation. It is this alienation which expressed itself as 'he never met a payroll,' he has long hair, too high a brow, or he is sinister and subversive. This alienation is the root of the decline of the Republican party."

"There is more than a grain of truth," wrote Malcolm C. Moos in *The Republicans,* "in the assertion that a large part of the leadership of the Republican party is anti-intellectual to the point of keeping out of its councils valuable human resources of men and women not only dedicated to the Republican party but often in key positions to keep a dynamic interest in Republicanism alive in the nation's intellectual centers."

"What I envy about our opposition," said Val Bjornson in a memorandum to the chairman of the Republican National Committee after he had been defeated for the Senate in Minnesota in 1954, "is the host of vigorous recruits it gets from the intelligent, aggressive, college-trained age bracket. . . . We need aggressive, intelligent, and devoted educated youth. . . ."

"People in distinctive language-culture groups frequently are sensitive about what sometimes seems to them to be Republican lack of interest in them except during the last hours of campaign vote-solicitation," said the Republican Committee on Big City Politics in a report to the Republican National Committee on January 2, 1962. "They sometimes assert that the Republican party is not interested in the working class to which most of them belong. This attitude, needless to say, has been cultivated by the Democrats."

"I've always assumed I was a Republican, but they've made such a mess of their party I'm ashamed to say I'm a Republican," a young farm wife near Freeport, Illinois, told pollster Samuel Lubell during the Johnson-Goldwater campaign. "From now on I'll register independent."

"Apparently," Governor Scranton said in commenting on the Johnson victory, "many Americans during the recent campaign gained the impression the Republican party was opposed or indifferent to so-called ethnic or minority groups. I found this impression deeply embedded in many cases."

"As long as the leaders of minority groups are denied the equality of opportunity which is supposedly the central core of the Republican party's philosophy, and as long as the Republican party is led and supported by those who actually mean equality and opportunity only for those like themselves," writes E. Digby Baltzell in *The Protestant Establishment*, "it is only natural, and an expression of their sense of

117

dignity, that minority-group leaders and their followers should continue to support the Democratic party."

"Our party has been more concerned that people can just keep what they've got," a former Republican national chairman told me recently. "People like to daydream—daydream about a second car, a bigger house, a week at the beach. The Democrats hold out hope to people who daydream. The Republicans give you the impression that if you have got fifty thousand dollars in the bank, by God, we're going to see to it that you still have fifty thousand dollars. The Democrats are going to see to it that you have more."

Historians, politicians, sociologists, pollsters, journalists, and assorted political pundits have been examining the sick Republican elephant almost every four years now for nearly a generation to find out what ails him. No one yet knows what medicine to prescribe, but at least the diagnosis is fairly much the same year after year. In layman's terms it runs like this: The Republicans are stand-patters, the party of the status quo. They have never really eliminated fear that they would turn back the clock. At heart they are really the party of the WASPS—the White Anglo-Saxon Protestants. They do not really like foreign accents, and they were as cold to the immigration of Puerto Ricans in the 1950's, as they had been to the arrival of the Irish in the 1850's.

The Republicans, so the diagnosis runs, cannot shake off their heritage as the rich man's party, the party of big business. "The Republicans may rejoice in the memory of Lincoln," Professor Rossiter wrote several years ago, "but if Lincoln were here today he would have had a hard time warming to a single man in Eisenhower's Cabinet."

A man with a great fund of common sense remarked during Senator Goldwater's acceptance speech at San Francisco, "He's knocking them dead out here, but what do you suppose this stuff sounds like outside the Cow Palace?" So what was new?

In 1936 Alf Landon carried two states—but what had the

Republicans said at the convention in Cleveland when they nominated him? "Re-man the citadels of liberty . . . Monstrous, reckless propaganda machine . . . Economic freedom . . . Coddles agitators . . . Siamese twins of bureaucracy . . . Un-American . . . Lavish spending . . . Unconstitutional dictatorship . . . Arrogant individual of Franklin Delano Roosevelt . . . New Deal spoilers and wasters . . . Never known the necessity of meeting a payroll . . . Thou shalt not steal . . . Tugwell . . . Wallace . . . Ickes . . . Plowed under the land of plenty . . . Boondoggled . . . Reciprocal-trade acts . . . NRA . . . AAA . . . Theory of the Old World . . . Planned economy . . . Economic blunders . . . New Deal pump primers . . . America is in peril . . . Valley Forge . . ."

It is nearly impossible to imagine how a convention could have met at that point in American history and said so many things that were so meaningless to so many people. It may have warmed the cockles of the heart of New York's then conservative Westchester County, but as one editor scored it when the Roosevelt-Landon returns were in on election night: "Country Club, 2—Country, 46."

During much of this generation there has been a gap between what the Republican party has been saying and what the people have been thinking. Somehow or other it has been impossible for the hard-core conservative faction of the party to grasp that the voters approve of the basic reforms of the New Deal and that although newer and better ideas may supplant these reforms, mere partisan invective will not exorcise them.

For years the Republican party has been misreading the times. As Mayer pointed out, it misread them in the 1920's, when it did not provide for the welfare of the masses, including the foreign-born and the Negroes moving into the cities. It misread them in the 1930's, when it leveled broadsides against Social Security, the wages-and-hours law, public housing, and other Depression measures. It misread them in the 1940's, when it voted against lend-lease and the extension of selective service. Certainly it misread the times in 1964, when it nominated for President a senator who had voted against the civil-rights act at a time when the overriding domestic issue in America was the movement to do justice to the Negroes.

The Republican performance over the last thirty years is that of a party that does not quite understand what it is that the American people have in their hearts and minds. In other words, Republicans address themselves too exclusively to Republicans. They are too eager to say what other Republicans want to hear. Senator Goldwater's campaign was the classic example of this failing. Night after night he would enter halls packed with ardent Goldwater followers and send them into delighted paroxysms with his attacks on the spenders and the demagogues. Day after day he would appear at airport rallies of well-dressed suburbanites and up-and-coming young business executives and beguile them with the doctrine of states' rights and the failings of the Supreme Court. But beyond appearances of this type there was but little effort to speak to the people, to appeal to those who had not been persuaded long ago. The contrast between the all-white audiences who listened to Goldwater and the crowds of Negroes who surrounded President Johnson in Baltimore, Macon, Jacksonville, Hartford, and other cities was astonishing.

The last thirty years abound in examples of how the Republican party has just missed being on the same wavelength as the people. Think of the Republican lungs that were worn out denouncing Eleanor Roosevelt. The Republicans seem fated to make little mistakes that jar public opinion at the wrong moment. For example, did Dewey have to administer a public bawling-out to the engineer of his whistle-stop train when it suddenly backed toward a crowd in Beaucoup, Illinois, in 1948? How silly it was for Richard Nixon, in the midst of a televised debate with Kennedy in

1960, to rise to moral indignation over Harry Truman's cursing. The Republicans have lacked the sense of humor that the Democrats have had. And another case of being out of step with public opinion occurred late on election night, when Goldwater went off to bed without conceding defeat when it was beyond question. People expect to see the loser jump over the net and shake hands after the match.

The Republicans love to play to vocal minorities. To be sure, it was fair game for them to make a political extravaganza out of the return of General Douglas MacArthur in 1951 after he had been relieved of his command by Truman. But the howls of protest in which the Republicans reveled were almost certainly not coming from the majority of the people. The majority of the people do not want a general who is bigger than the President of the United States any more than do the historians, who have now, by and large, vindicated Truman's decision.

The modern history of the Republican party is all too full of histrionics staged for the benefit of the vocal minority and all too short of appeals to the larger and less vocal groups and interests that make up the majority of the electorate. As a result the party has long had an inadequate base. The Goldwater strategy made a bad situation worse by concentrating on a sectional victory, pieced together with the South and several other states. A candidate who practically wrote off the industrial Northeast and who spent as much time talking to Birmingham as to New York City was working from much too narrow a base to provide a party with great national power. After election day Thruston Morton put his finger on the trouble when he said that the Republican party must seek "a more cosmopolitan structure and outlook."

11

ANY ATTEMPT to arrive at an understanding of the Republican predicament today must begin with a recognition that in a period of revolutionary change both in this country and around the world the party has not kept pace.

The lag that began in the Taft administration grew seriously in the 1920's, when the Republican leaders failed to understand that a new order was coming in the wake of World War I. When the old order collapsed, late in the decade, they were unprepared for it. As the new order began taking root in the 1930's they still clung to the old. And now for the last quarter of a century the party has been declining. In 1940, according to Gallup, thirty-eight percent of American adults considered themselves Republicans, but in 1964 only twenty-five percent did.

This retrogression is in part a reflection of the fact that in a time of such tremendous revolutionary changes as the twentieth century has produced, institutions that do not keep abreast falter and decline. Change is the law of life. The Ecumenical Council offers a dramatic example of how such an old and conservative institution as the Roman Catholic Church can reform itself and bring itself more into harmony with the modern age. Catholics who lived even a generation ago could not have believed possible the transformations that have been wrought during the sessions in Rome over the past three years.

The Republican party was somewhat modernized under

Eisenhower, but the pace and scope of its reformation and modernization have lagged well behind the requirements of an America well into the second half of the twentieth century.

For too long the Republicans equated true conservatism with business conservatism, as if there were no conservative philosophy other than that enunciated by the National Association of Manufacturers. President Coolidge captured the spirit of his administration all too well when he said, "The business of America is business." His contemporaries would have profited by paying more attention to the elder Henry Cabot Lodge, who said, "The businessman dealing with a large political question is really a painful sight."

Because so many Republican leaders of the last thirty years have longed to return to the good old days, they have miscalculated the number of voters who would like to follow them, as Senator Goldwater has been the latest to learn.

"The average American has no great nostalgia for the past," Professor Andrew Hacker of Cornell University ventured to write recently. "For many indeed the 'good old days' were marked by existence of urban slums or rural poverty, by economic exploitation and limited educational advantages. For this reason there is no great impetus to move the clock back, to repeal existing legislation, or to try to simplify the complexities of modern government."

Republican Presidential candidates like Willkie, Dewey, Eisenhower, and Nixon were well aware of this. In long stretches when the party has been out of power, however, its most numerous spokesmen between Presidential campaigns have been Republicans in Congress who more often than not exaggerated the party's conservative bent. Coming—many of them—from small towns and rural areas, their pronouncements frequently had a reactionary ring out of tune with the feelings and needs of masses of voters in large cities. Off and on for years some of the most piercing voices on Capitol Hill were those of Midwestern Republicans attacking measures designed to help city dwellers. Time and again they—and even Republicans of greater stature—have conveyed the idea that they feared change of any kind. Their fear was often contacted from unprogressive business constituents to whom any federal regulation was abhorrent.

Among the several revolutionary changes in American life that the Republican leaders of the 1920's failed at their peril to grasp was the fact that they were witnessing, so far as it is possible to judge today, the sunset of white Anglo-Saxon Protestant domination of the American political scene. They did not perceive that the new generations of Negroes and the Germans, Swedes, Irish, and Poles and other Eastern Europeans, taken together, were contending with the old stock for political supremacy. White, rural, small-town, Protestant Americans no longer represented the majority, even though the Republican leaders shut their eyes to the change. Of the two hundred and sixteen federal judges appointed in the twelve years of Harding, Coolidge, and Hoover, only sixteen were Catholic or Jewish.

"Between the crash in 1929 and the landslide election of 1936," says Baltzell in his new book, *The Protestant Establishment,* "the Democrats, under the leadership of Franklin Roosevelt, became the majority party in a nation increasingly composed of an urban and ethnically mixed electorate whose aspirations were more likely to be expressed in collective and political terms, largely because many of them were denied access to success at the core of the business and corporate power structure."

The causes of the Republican decline were uncomfortably like the causes of the disappearance of the Federalist party, chief among which were that it was a "nativist" party in a country already burgeoning with immigrants and that it was an anti-popular party in a country over which political and social democracy was sweeping in waves.

"The Old Federalists," wrote Professor Denis Brogan of Cambridge University, "had been more of the temper of

124

Coriolanus; even when they wooed the plebs, they did it ungracefully and unconvincingly." And as Rossiter comments, "An American party must woo the plebs wholeheartedly or go out of business."

In the 1920's the Republicans ignored the deprivations of the Negroes, who had been Republican voters since the Civil War. It was perfectly natural, therefore, that in the 1930's the majority of Negroes moved over to the shelter of the New Deal, which provided them food, jobs, housing, a glimmer of hope, and even a promise of dignity. President Eisenhower might have led them back by championing the Supreme Court's decision on public-school segregation. He did not do this, however. More recently Goldwater sealed them off from the Republican party for an unforeseeable period, perhaps a generation, by his vote against the civil-rights bill and the racist character of his campaign in the South. Thus, having long ago lost the labor vote, the Republicans have now deprived themselves of the vote of the Negroes, of whom, it has been estimated, nearly six million were registered in 1964.

The election of a Catholic Democratic President in 1960 was a culmination of social and political changes, changes that have been creeping up on the Republicans unnoticed for at least a generation. That election, close as it was, underscored the Democrats' understanding of the forces that have changed this century.

It is difficult to glimpse into the next decade. But the country is prosperous; there is more to conserve than ever before; a feeling of some magnitude exists that it may be time to slow down a bit and digest the revolutionary changes of the past. Having failed to control the liberal period from 1932 onward, it would be a strange fate for the Republicans if they are unable to rule during a conservative period that may be setting in. President Johnson, though he is not likely to surrender the main liberal programs, has nevertheless the skill to accommodate this point of view. After all, he was

125

regarded by millions as a truer conservative than Goldwater. No one is more aware than the President that he received a large conservative vote. Notwithstanding medical care for the elderly, extension of the anti-poverty program, and several others, Johnson may camp on so much conservative territory that the Republicans will have a hard time pitching their tents anywhere near the center for years.

It is not easy to be the party long out of power. If the Republicans simply say they can do what the Democrats have been doing but can do it better, this is in a sense "me-tooism," as Goldwater charged. But the opposite course, which Goldwater followed, produced negative results. Listening to the senator on the hustings it was hard to imagine what vision his audiences were carrying away. It was never difficult to imagine what visions President Kennedy's audiences carried away, nor President Johnson's, for that matter.

"So here's the Great Society," he said in a campaign speech in Pittsburgh. "It's the time—and it's going to be soon—when nobody in this country is poor. It's the time—and there's no point in waiting—when every boy or girl can have all the education that boy or girl can put to good use. It's the time when there is a job for everybody who wants to work. It's the time when every slum is gone from every city in America, and America is beautiful. It's the time when man gains full domination under God over his own destiny. It's the time of peace on earth and goodwill among men." The details, as *Time* magazine noted, were left to be filled in, but one candidate at least was offering a vision.

In the comparative public sophistication of these times the conservative Republicans are gaining no ground by being everlastingly anti-government. The British Conservative party has done fairly well without this dogma. Certainly the federal government can no longer govern as it did in McKinley's day. After his defeat in 1948, Dewey had some grounds for grumbling when he said, "It must have been some very clumsy Republican—I do not know the origin of the phrase or who perpetrated it—who tried to pin the label 'Welfare State' on Mr. Truman's government. But others joined in the clamor and, of course, the apologists for Big Government joyously accepted the epithet as a new instrument of party warfare. They admit they are running a welfare state. There has never been a responsible government which did not have the welfare of its people at heart. I am proud of the fact that we in the state of New York have made great social welfare advances, as have most of the states."

At some time—and somewhere between the scylla of "metooism" and the charybdis of negativism—the Republican party is going to have to find a vision to hold out to the American people in the second half of the twentieth century.

12

WHAT ABOUT THE FUTURE of the Republican party?
For perspective on its current travail, let us go back momentarily to two of the GOP's worst hours in this century
and in their bleak light ask the same question: "What is the
future of the Republican party?"

The first occasion was the morning after the election of
1912. A calamitous defeat had befallen the party that had
controlled the White House for forty-four of the previous
fifty-two years, dating back to Lincoln's first inauguration.
That summer of 1912, however, Theodore Roosevelt,
"strong as a bull moose," had stood at Armageddon, done
battle for the Lord, and led the Progressives out of the Republican convention in Chicago that had renominated
President Taft.

An amputated Republican party went to the polls, and
when the electoral votes were counted, Wilson received
four hundred and thirty-five, Roosevelt eighty-eight, and
Taft eight. What future was there for a party that had received eight electoral votes? In 1916 the Republicans met
again in Chicago with a rather standard array of contenders: former Vice-President Charles W. Fairbanks, Senators
John W. Weeks of Massachusetts, William E. Borah of
Idaho, and Albert B. Cummins of Iowa, and former Senators Elihu Root of New York and Theodore Burton of Ohio.

Passing over all of them, the convention nominated
Charles Evans Hughes of New York, an associate justice of

the Supreme Court. That fall, just four years after Taft had received eight electoral votes, Hughes almost defeated Wilson. The electoral vote: Wilson two hundred and seventy-seven, Hughes two hundred and fifty-four. Wilson barely squeaked through by virtue of a plurality of a few thousand votes in California. Four years later, in 1920, the Republicans returned to the White House.

The next occasion in question was the morning after the election of 1936. Though the *Literary Digest* poll had predicted that Governor Landon of Kansas would win, President Roosevelt carried every state in the Union except Maine and Vermont. Considering that the Republicans were already something of a national joke at the time, what possible future was there for a party that could win only two small states?

Nevertheless they showed up for their convention in Philadelphia in 1940. The roster of prospective candidates included the obvious ones: Taft of Ohio, Vandenberg of Michigan, Dewey of New York, and Martin of Massachusetts (a dark horse). It was a scorching fight for five ballots. On the sixth, Wendell Willkie ran away with it. He waged a tremendous campaign, one of the most exciting of modern times. He did not win, but his twenty-two million votes redeemed the memory of 1936.

Even in its most disheartening defeats, then, the Republican party has shown extraordinary recuperative powers. Following the humiliations of 1912 and 1936, moreover, the party turned away from the obvious office seekers and nominated strong candidates chosen from unlikely sources. In 1916 it plucked Hughes from the Supreme Court and in 1940 it reached into the financial community for Willkie, a Democrat of recent vintage. These examples suggest that the destiny of the Republican party in the wake of the Goldwater debacle is not necessarily tied to any of the shopworn names that will keep appearing in the headlines for the next two or three years. If the party succeeds in climbing out of the ruins of 1964, as it has done in the past, its nominee in 1968 may be as unusual a choice as Hughes in 1916 and Willkie in 1940. But first the ruins must be surmounted.

If the Republicans are to be, or merely seem to be, the voice of right-wing radicalism or extremism, advocating reactionary changes at home and adventures abroad that might lead to war, they will remain a minority party indefinitely. Whom they nominate will not make any great difference.

But if they swing back as the conservative party of the center, standing in opposition to the Democrats as the liberal party of the center, nothing in the 1964 election returns foredooms them to permanent minority status.

Although it is hard to exaggerate their difficulties, the Republicans are better off in important respects than they were after the ravages of 1936. Despite the Johnson landslide, they have been left with more positions of power at the top. Thus they begin their climb back from defeat from a base that includes roughly one third of the Senate, one third of the House of Representatives, and one third of the governors. The Republican governors are a capable group that is already taking steps to put the party back on its feet and lead it toward more familiar ground.

On the other hand, below the top layer of power the Republicans have been hurt as badly as or worse than they were in 1936. In 1964 the Democrats won clear control of thirty-two state legislatures, seven more than before. In six other states where the Republicans had majorities in both houses of the legislature, the Democrats captured one house or the other.

"In thirty-six we didn't get hit so hard at the local level," a former Republican national chairman said in assaying the 1964 returns. "It was murderous—the councilmen, the county officials, and the legislators we lost this year. The courthouse damage to the Republican party has just been tremendous. Nothing like it. A broom that swept all away. When the Democrats took the New York legislature we lost a million dollars' worth of jobs. And that doesn't tell the story of the carnage in the counties. It's incredible, but the Democrats carried every county in New York State. To give you an idea of what that means, in Nassau County we lost two hundred and twenty-five jobs in the sheriff's office alone."

In terms of national restoration the power they retain at the top is more important to the Republicans than the local offices they lost. But of course there is an interrelationship between the two. It is more than a cliche that the Republicans will have to begin rebuilding from the communities up. The time has come for the party to concentrate less on ideology and more on votes. "It may be," as a *Wall Street Journal* editorial said after the election, "that the Republicans have been too long in love with ideology for practical electoral purposes; they tend to carry their splits to the point of weakening their effectiveness at the polls. They certainly did this time."

The Republicans are at a disadvantage in possessing no powerful auxiliary such as the Democrats have in the Committee on Political Education (COPE). In many areas COPE wins elections for the Democrats with the assistance of its funds and its efforts to get people to the polls to register and vote. For years Republican registration drives have been notoriously inadequate.

"It's easy to get Republicans interested in getting out the vote on election day," a Midwestern Republican state chairman told me during the campaign, "but they aren't so interested in getting out to register. They forget that if you aren't registered you're a dead duck on election day."

Johnson's sweep of the cities and suburbs points to where the Republicans' largest task lies. They cannot hope to return to power until they begin winning there. Nixon too ran poorly in the cities in 1960, and as a result the Republican

131

National Committee commissioned a study, which, though seemingly ignored in 1964, to the party's misfortune, still offers good advice on how to proceed. The study was made in 1961 by the Republican Committee on Big City Politics, which was headed by Ray C. Bliss, Republican state chairman of Ohio and one of the party's ablest organizers. The purpose was to plan how the Republicans could recapture the big-city vote, and many of the programs could be applied to the suburban vote as well.

Bliss placed great stress on year-round precinct work under the supervision of full-time, paid professional staffs. It does, incidentally, seem to be quite true that the Democrats take a good deal more pride than their opponents in political professionalism, which is something that the Republicans would be wise to emulate.

The late David Lloyd George, former Prime Minister of Great Britain, once remarked that what the United States needed was not more statesmen but more good politicians; in its present stage this is a prime need of the Republican party.

Naturally, in view of the party's unsatisfactory showing for many years past, the Bliss report made a point of the necessity for registration of more voters. It set certain standards for fund raising and recruiting, but perhaps its most important emphasis was on the necessity for the Republicans to work with all groups in the cities—ethnic minorities and labor as well as business tycoons and those easily identifiable young types in Republican gatherings who dream of being tycoons.

"The regular Republican organization in predominantly Negro wards in our big cities," said Bliss in words that deserved more attention in 1964, "frequently is woefully weak and just as frequently nonexistent. Our problem in these situations is to establish effective personal contacts within the Negro community and draw Negro citizens into regular party activities."

132

And here is another point Bliss made that might profitably be listened to now: "The Republican party will be a minority in the big cities until its true concern with the problems of all citizens is accurately and fully identified. Our party is too frequently mistakenly identified with big business and privilege. . . . The Republican party must fight being erroneously labeled as the party which is against change and new ideas."

As the election recedes into the past, the outlines of the future of the Republican party are coming into clearer focus.

A strong pull back toward the center is being exerted through the power points of the party—the Republican governors, professionals, members of the Senate and House, and national leaders such as Eisenhower and Nixon. The election returns proved to be very sobering. The rashness of the venture of trying to win with an extreme conservative and the discouragement resulting from a long string of failures with "me-to" candidates are apparent to the party professionals.

Increasingly their attitude is that the right wing had its chance with its most attractive candidate and that in light of the disastrous results the party must move back to its old ground. The folly of the Goldwater nomination has sunk in. Republicans must campaign as a modern party, and many of those who may not have realized this before realize it now. It has become clearer that the party must make a distinction between the conservatism represented by Senator Goldwater and his supporters and the conservatism that conserves.

Republican leaders are coming to accept the message implied in the election returns—that in times of peace and prosperity the American people do not wish to be confronted with a choice between extremes. The lesson that the election taught about the need for the party to be a party of broad consensus was partly responsible for the

133

sharp reaction among Republicans against Goldwater's post-election statement on political realignment.

There was no significant backing in the party for the senator's suggestion at Montego Bay, Jamaica, that "The time has come to choose up two new teams and get going." In his view the Democrats should become the party of the liberals and the Republicans the party of the conservatives. Instead of winning any support for this radical proposal, Goldwater merely strengthened the impression that he had not grasped the meaning of the election returns.

In the movement now under way to restore the party there is a strong feeling that instead of handing over its liberal and moderate elements to the Democrats, the Republicans cannot afford to write off any groups or interests whatever. On the contrary, it must broaden its appeal to include all voters, including the Negroes and the ethnic minorities mentioned in the Bliss report.

In seeking to halt the drift of voters away from the party that has been taking place for the last twenty-five years, the first task is to bring back the millions of Republicans who voted for Johnson and the other millions who rebuked the party for the Goldwater nomination by staying home on election day, at the same time managing to hold the millions who favored the nomination of Goldwater.

This will be difficult to do. However, the Democrats manage, for example, to keep Senator James O. Eastland of Mississippi and Senator Joseph S. Clark of Pennsylvania in the same party. The Republicans will have to make similar accommodations of their own—and without too much delay. If the millions of Republicans who either voted for Johnson or stayed home should desert their party in another Presidential election, the party's future would become much more precarious than it is today.

There is no reason for despair over the Republicans' chances of regaining a degree of unity comparable to that which existed at the time of the Nixon campaign. Achieving this will require new leadership. The liberals and moderates will not follow anyone who had a part in advancing Senator Goldwater, and millions of sincere Goldwater followers would probably turn their backs on someone such as Lindsay, even if he were meantime elected governor of New York. Although the leader who is needed has yet to come forward, time may take care of this; perhaps it will become clear who this leader is to be as a result of the 1966 congressional elections. A dramatic victory by Charles H. Percy over Senator Paul H. Douglas in Illinois, for example, might give the Republicans a Presidential candidate that the quarreling factions could support. Because younger candidates such as Percy and Taft were defeated in 1964 in a national landslide for which they were in no way responsible, their political careers are not necessarily ended. Taft is forty-seven, Percy forty-five.

Many Republicans, in considering ways of restoring the party's strength, have realized that the South is still a land of opportunity for them—but not the South as represented by Alabama and Mississippi in their present stage of development. The Republican party cannot rebuild on the basis of the hard-core South that Goldwater carried and still hope to win national elections. The Republicans must forget about Governor Wallace and return to the appeal to the progressive areas of the South that stood Eisenhower and Nixon in good stead.

In spite of Johnson's victory in most of the Southern states in 1964, the national policies that the Democrats have followed since the New Deal and will continue to pursue have cost them their monopoly of the South.

The old regional loyalty to the Democrats can never be restored to what it was, any more perhaps than the old rock-ribbed steadfastness of the past can be restored for the Republicans in northern New England.

The Republican party is sinking its roots gradually deeper into Southern soil. When even Georgia goes Republican, as it did for the first time in 1964, it is a sign that old psychological barriers against leaving the Democratic party are breaking down.

Almost as important as what has happened in the Presidential elections is the fact that more and more Republicans are running in the South for congressional seats and for state, county, and local offices. Only a relatively few of them have won so far, but in many cases their share of the vote is rising. Though he was defeated by Governor Orval Faubus in Arkansas in 1964, for example, Winthrop Rockefeller received 42.6 percent of the popular vote. This surely is a solid basis on which the Republicans can build in the future. The men who will in time get control of the party will shift the appeal in the South away from racism and back to economic conservatism.

The return to a stronger position on civil rights that is foreshadowed in the Republican reaction to the 1964 defeat will drive away those newly won Southern supporters, who are an embarrassment to the party nationally.

An early step in the rebuilding process, whose need is now widely recognized in the party, is for the Republicans to offer a reasonably constructive opposition in Congress. A prerequisite is to recognize the 1964 defeat for what it was and not fall into the defeatism that in the late 1940's and early 1950's produced the McCarthy era. This would only add another huge obstacle on the already difficult road back to power.

Since they cannot easily obstruct the President in Congress because of their reduced numbers, the worst tactics for the Republicans would be to seem obstructionist. Criticism that is intelligent, forceful, and fair is their best course. Before long there will be many issues for them to develop.

As a result of the 1964 landslide, which has for the time being reduced the effectiveness of the two-party system, the American people will be sensitive to any sign of abuse of powers by the President. There are already grounds for searching questions about United States policy in Southeast Asia. A federal budget of more than one hundred billion dollars will contain many expenditures open to question. The Republicans will do well too to give careful scrutiny to the efficacy of such large new ventures as the antipoverty program. Is it really going to reduce poverty, or is it so much pork barrel? Is there a better way to go about the problem of attacking poverty?

The Republicans in Congress will surely waste no time in beginning to pry away at the unusual coalition that supported President Johnson against Goldwater. Some of these groups have deeply conflicting interests that are bound to be affected one way or another by decisions the President will have to make someday. With all his skill he will have a difficult time holding the loyalty of groups hurt by these decisions. Disaffected elements of the Johnson coalition will be fair game for the Republicans.

The role of constructive criticism is probably a better course for the Republicans now than an attempt to produce a broad national program of their own. For some time to come the party will be too divided to be able to agree on a program that would have a strong national appeal. The party's weakness in this respect is underscored by the nature of its leadership in the House of Representatives.

Charles Halleck, the floor leader, comes from Rensselaer, Indiana. Leslie C. Arends, the minority whip, comes from Melville, Illinois. John W. Byrnes, chairman of the Republican Policy Committee, comes from Green Bay, Wisconsin. Powerful but nontitled Republican leaders such as Gerald R. Ford and Clarence J. Brown come, respectively, from Grand Rapids, Michigan, and Blanchester, Ohio. These districts are not likely wellsprings of programs that will appeal to voters jammed into teeming cities and sprawling suburbs.

"The air is very pure in Blanchester," a Washington observer said recently. "The people out there don't want to pay taxes for air-pollution programs. They don't like mass transit, and they don't see any reason why they should have to pay for it. They won't have their congressman vote that way."

If strong enough collective leadership can be exerted in the early stages of the party's reconstruction to keep factional quarrels from doing even greater damage to the Republicans' structure and image, the party could become an arena of excitement and clashing ideas. A few weeks after the election a professor at Harvard told me that for the first time in his life he and many of his colleagues were concerned about the Republican party. "We used to look down our noses at it," he said, "but now there is a great deal of interest in seeing it built back up for the sake of the country."

A genuine debate in the party over principles and policies would attract able minds. It could provide a climate for much-needed reformation and modernization. In fact, the Republican party could be much more interesting in the next four years than the Democratic party, blanketed by the Johnson administration. The primary objective of the Republicans now is a creditable showing in the 1966 congressional elections, and history will be on their side, since the party out of power usually gains Senate and House seats in off-year elections. The challenge of 1966 will help the Republicans get back on their feet. It is easier for the party to unite for a congressional election than for a Presidential election, when, as often happens, the fight over the nomination drains off the enthusiasm of the losing side.

The vitality of the American system is such that the Republican party, all but shattered in 1964, could give President Johnson a stiff fight in 1968. This could come about through the rise of a dynamic leader capable of catching the fancy of the people at a moment of boredom with the Johnson administration. It could come about as a result of Democratic blunders or scandals or as a result of some catastrophe abroad or serious misfortune at home such as serious inflation or a serious recession. In 1968, after eight years of Democratic rule, the voters might simply feel the time has come for a change.

Although this is entirely possible, it is not probable. The Republicans have missed too many opportunities, have had too much bad luck, and have spent too much time fighting among themselves and too little time thinking about the problems of the twentieth century to return to power so soon. Although they are not necessarily condemned to permanent minority status, they will probably remain a minority for some years until they—or until events—offer Democrats and independent voters a compelling reason for deserting the Democratic party. The Democrats have all but crowded the Republicans off the main positions of the day. It will take time for the Republicans to recover them or develop new positions that will attract a majority of voters.

As the minority party for some time to come the Republicans can still be a vital force in American life. The challenge they face in returning to the eminent position they once occupied, however, is an appallingly difficult one.